The Project

This volume contains the summary reports of two distinguished panels—one from the United States and one from Western Europe—on the separate, parallel studies they have conducted over the past several years on approaches to preventing the spread of nuclear weapons to additional countries. The purposes of having parallel studies by the two groups were to identify similarities and differences in their perception of the proliferation problem and how best to approach it; to help stimulate greater West European interest in this important international security problem and improve the coordination of West European policies in this field; to increase U.S. sensitivity to European points of view on this subject; and generally to encourage a more effective common approach to non-proliferation among the Atlantic partners.

Selected supporting papers from each study are being published separately.

The studies, conducted under the aegis of the Council of Foreign Relations and the Centre for European Policy Studies, respectively, were made possible by generous grants from the Ford Foundation, the Rockefeller Brothers Fund, and (in the case of the U.S. study) the McKnight Foundation and an individual donor. For a description of the proceedings of the two panels and acknowledgements of the valuable contributions of others, see Appendix I.

The members of the two panels are listed below, with fuller identification in Appendix J.

The U.S. Panel

Gerard C. Smith
Robert A. Charpie
Alton Frye
J. Robert Schaetzel
L. Dean Brown
Albert Carnesale
Warren Christopher
John Hugh Crimmins
Warren Donnelly
Philip J. Farley
Ellen Frost
Mark Garrison

William Gleysteen
Robert Goheen
Benjamin Huberman
Spurgeon M. Keeny, Jr.
Andrew Pierre
Robert V. Roosa
James R. Schlesinger
Brent Scowcroft
Marshall Shulman
Samuel F. Wells
Charles N. Van Doren

The European Panel

Johan Jørgen Holst
Sergio Finzi
David Fischer
Bertrand Goldschmidt
Simone Herpels
Guenter Hildenbrand
Giorgio La Malfa
Peter Ludlow
Sir Ronald Mason
Angel Viñas
Harald Müller

BLOCKING
THE SPREAD OF
NUCLEAR
WEAPONS

American and European Perspectives

PUBLISHED IN COOPERATION WITH THE
CENTRE FOR EUROPEAN POLICY STUDIES (CEPS)

COUNCIL ON FOREIGN RELATIONS

COUNCIL ON FOREIGN RELATIONS BOOKS

The Council on Foreign Relations, Inc., is a nonprofit and nonpartisan organization devoted to promoting improved understanding of international affairs through the free exchange of ideas. The Council does not take any position on questions of foreign policy and has no affiliation with, and receives no funding from, the United States government.

From time to time, books and monographs written by members of the Council's research staff or visiting fellows, or commissioned by the Council, or written by an independent author with critical review contributed by a Council study or working group are published with the designation "Council on Foreign Relations Book." Any book or monograph bearing that designation is, in the judgment of the Committee on Studies of the Council's board of directors, a responsible treatment of a significant international topic worthy of presentation to the public. All statements of fact and expressions of opinion contained in Council books are, however, the sole responsibility of the author.

Copyright © 1986 by the Council on Foreign Relations, Inc.
All rights reserved.
Printed in the United States of America

© Copyright 1985, Centre for European Policy Studies. All rights reserved.

Library of Congress Cataloging-in-Publication Data

Blocking the spread of nuclear weapons.

   "Published in cooperation with the Centre for European Policy Studies, CEPS."
   1. Nuclear nonproliferation.   I.   Council on Foreign Relations.   II.   Centre for European Policy Studies (Louvain-la-Neuve, Belgium)
JX1974.73.B55   1986   327.1'74   86-4196
ISBN 0-87609-012-9

Contents

Toward a common approach
A foreword by the Chairmen of the two panels

Some poetic justice may be found in that an imprecise word, non-proliferation, is matched by public inattention to a major and growing international danger. That a number of years have passed with no additions to the small group of nuclear weapons states lends currency to a complacently wrong conclusion that at least this one nuclear problem no longer needs priority attention.

The facts and the conclusion are in sharp conflict. For half a century the world has lived uneasily in the nuclear age. We now face an acceleration in the spread of technology, and the ranks of nuclear scientists and engineers multiply. Not merely the advanced nations but newly industrialized countries now produce and export components of the nuclear fuel cycle. The rapid approach of new technology, as in the critical area of isotopic separation, will make more accessible a capacity to produce weapon-grade material clandestinely and at modest cost.

The present international non-proliferation regime rests in part on explicit obligations of the superpowers to reduce their nuclear arsenals. Arms build-up rather than the promised arms reductions can only undermine this control regime. There is a relationship between non-proliferation and the role of nuclear weapons in the strategies of the Northern powers, and a need for them to reduce their reliance on nuclear weapons if they hope to succeed in persuading other states to continue indefinitely to forgo the nuclear option.

One conclusion we derive from our parallel studies is that America and Europe suffer from different strains of a common virus: cultural lag. During the early years of the nuclear age the United States was in effect the monopolist supplier of technology and of fuel for nuclear electric plants. Thus, for a time, it was possible for America to set the terms on which components and fuel could move internationally. Those days are long gone. Yet a worried and vocal minority in the U.S. Congress, ignoring changed realities, insists that nuclear proliferation can be controlled by a crusading American government armed with layers of American legislation. The European strain of this virus has been to attack the proliferation problem on an individual nation basis rather than to recognize that coordination and concerted policies are needed. There is also a need to co-opt key states from the South as partners in the management of a truly international non-proliferation regime. The American and European reports contained in this volume, in addition to analyses and conclusions, suggest ways of breaking out of these cultural restraints.

As leaders of these related but independent projects, each of us has been struck by the wide areas of trans-Atlantic agreement reached by our two panels. Where disagreement exists it is more nuance than substance.*

First, neither report sounds a doomsday alarm; each concludes that the chances for controlling proliferation lie in good part on building on the sound foundation of existing policies and institutional structures.

Second, the threat of nuclear proliferation is not a general phenomenon that menaces the world. It is specific, definable dangers in a limited number of countries. Each member of this small group of some dozen states has different motives, perceives a unique threat to its security or prestige, and has its own distinct nuclear capability. This leads to the conclusion that dissuasion of proliferation must go well beyond export controls, the international safeguards system, and the threat of sanctions, and recognize the utility of positive rewards from cooperation and of building on common interests. The incentives, attractions, and concerns that may appear to some states to make nuclear weapons an interesting option must be understood, and the regional tensions and basic security interests addressed. Potential proliferators need to be persuaded that the acquisition of nuclear weapons will not lead to national security—as the superpowers are now realizing.

Third, this leads to a related conclusion. If persuasion, a synonym for diplomacy, is essential, who will be the persuader? It is here that a substantial change in American attitudes must take place. Rather than lectures and threats delivered from Washington, effective persuasion is more likely to come from non-nuclear-weapon nations (such as Canada, Sweden, Japan, or some Euratom members) that had the obvious capability to become military nuclear powers but elected not to do so. It is in the context of active diplomacy that Europe and the United States must collaborate in engaging such third-party persuaders in this endeavor. This delicate diplomacy requires that the balance between cooperation and threats or sanctions be tilted toward the former. Furthermore, punitive actions or threats to this end have been overrated as effective instruments of policy.

* For a more detailed comparison of the two reports, see Appendix A.

Fourth, our intensive examination of the six states of greatest near-term concern—Pakistan, India, South Africa, Israel, Brazil and Argentina—led to the conclusion that the uneasy *status quo* would probably prevail for the next several years. A variety of restraints and inhibitions affect in different ways each of these nations—internal forces, the potential loss of foreign aid, the threat of sanctions, the risk of stimulating a regional nuclear arms race. Yet these are volatile situations and the risk of a lunge towards nuclear weapons is real.

Fifth, if proliferation is to be avoided, more than European-American collaboration is required. The existing cooperation among several major supplier states must be strengthened and extended, including drawing in new supplying nations. The role of the Soviet Union is also critical. Members of the American panel met with Soviet officials and experts brought together by the Soviet Academy of Sciences. The discussions in Moscow confirmed that the USSR assesses the proliferation problem about as we do. The importance of this common view should be underscored. It suggests continued Soviet support for the existing non-proliferation regime. They share as well our concern about new suppliers and new technology. And in view of the weight we give to regional tensions as the breeding ground for proliferation, the USSR must be involved in the search for ways of banking down these regions of potential crisis.

Finally, we stress the absence of any simple, assured remedy to the threat of nuclear proliferation. Rather, the nature of the threat demands responses as complex as the problem, and an extraordinary degree of international collaboration. The greatest present danger lies in South Asia and arises from fear and enmity that mark Pakistan-India relations, heightened by the alignment of the Soviet Union with India and that of China and the United States with Pakistan. If an overt nuclear race in South Asia or elsewhere is to be avoided, the nuclear powers concerned must develop coherent approaches. This means that concerted efforts to reduce the underlying regional tensions while at the same time making available resources designed to help the contending nations (with the obverse ability to withhold assistance) are part of a non-proliferation strategy.

In September 1985, 86 parties to the Non-Proliferation Treaty participated in their third review conference. The positive and constructive Final Declaration came as a surprise and offers hope for preserving and strengthening the existing non-proliferation regime. This is especially important because in 1995 the Treaty will need to be extended. Yet the conference also indicated a strong undercurrent of impatience in the member states over the lack of progress in arms control, especially the failure to negotiate a comprehensive test ban.

This leads us to conclude that while we have some time, it is only limited. It falls to Western Europe and the United States, working with other like-minded countries, to take the lead in supporting the existing international non-proliferation regime, and to ease the underlying political and security problems that could draw additional states into the military nuclear club. And finally, the *sine qua non* for success is real progress in arms control on the part of the nuclear superpowers.

Gerard C. Smith
Chairman, U.S. Panel

Johan Jørgen Holst
Chairman, European Steering Group

January 1986

BLOCKING
THE SPREAD OF
NUCLEAR
WEAPONS

American and European Perspectives

Containing Nuclear Proliferation: A New Assessment

Summary Report of the U.S. Panel on New Approaches to Non-Proliferation

Gerard C. Smith, Robert A. Charpie, Alton Frye,
J. Robert Schaetzel, L. Dean Brown, Albert Carnesale,
Warren Christopher, John Hugh Crimmins, Warren Donnelly,
Philip J. Farley, Ellen Frost, Mark Garrison, William Gleysteen,
Robert Goheen, Benjamin Huberman, Spurgeon M. Keeny, Jr.,
Andrew Pierre, Robert V. Roosa, James R. Schlesinger,
Brent Scowcroft, Marshall Shulman,
Samuel F. Wells, Charles N. Van Doren

Introduction

The risk of several additional countries acquiring nuclear weapons is clear and present. It is particularly acute in some of the world's most volatile areas where the addition of a nuclear dimension to regional hostilities could have disastrous consequences.

Pakistan's obvious pursuit of a nuclear weapons capability may cause India to revive its nuclear explosive program after an apparent hiatus since 1974. This could lead Pakistan to go even further, and a regional nuclear arms race would be underway. The Indians could readily outpace the Pakistanis, but probably not match the Chinese, who might help Pakistan (though such help now seems less likely than heretofore). Future hostilities in the area could then result in the actual use of nuclear weapons, with appalling loss of life, and might escalate into a broader conflict involving the superpowers.

The latter possibility is potentially greater in the Middle East. Although Israel's nuclear capabilities are currently unmatched in the area, they seem likely in the longer run to provoke the acquisition of nuclear weapons by her adversaries—or at least a demand by them for Soviet nuclear backing.

Such possibilities highlight the need for a fresh assessment of the problem of containing further proliferation and of the relative efficacy of different approaches thereto, with emphasis on how they affect the countries closest to acquiring nuclear weapons.

The challenge is formidable. Technical barriers to proliferation are diminishing. A number of countries are acquiring the requisite nuclear materials and other technical capabilities; and technologies now under development may make the acquisition of weapons-usable materials easier and the task of safeguarding against their misuse more difficult. Several states have deliberately avoided non-proliferation commitments and international safeguards on key parts of their nuclear programs, and appear determined to make nuclear weapons, or at least to establish and maintain the option to do so. Advocates of nuclear weapons can point to:

— the international status, prestige, and bargaining power of the nuclear weapon states;

— the apparent success and stability—thus far—of mutual nuclear deterrence in the East-West context; and

— the French nuclear arsenal as an example of deterrence based on a numerically inferior nuclear force.

Moreover, they can argue that existing legal and political barriers to proliferation may prove fragile.

But there is still a reasonable chance that further proliferation can be avoided, or at least contained, and that even in the most worrisome cases major steps towards nuclear weaponry—such as nuclear weapons testing—can be headed off.

So far, the spread of nuclear weapons has been much slower than predicted. In the past two decades, only one clearly established nuclear explosion by a country not previously considered a nuclear weapon state has occurred—the Indian explosion in 1974—and that does not appear to have been followed by the build-up of a nuclear arsenal. The acquisition of the special materials and technology needed to make nuclear weapons has not, in most cases, led to decisions to make such weapons. In fact, most of the advanced industrial countries that clearly have such capabilities—including states such as Canada, Sweden, Japan, and the European NATO countries other than France and the United Kingdom—have thus far determined that it would be against their interest to acquire nuclear weapons and have joined in international non-proliferation commitments reflecting and reenforcing that determination. There is a growing awareness of the local and global risks of recourse to nuclear war and the questionable military utility of nuclear weapons, and it is no longer considered self-evident that "going nuclear" enhances a nation's security or political standing. These new insights were reflected in the outcome of the 1985 NPT Review Conference (discussed in Appendix C).

*   *   *

This summary report advocates building on the existing international consensus against proliferation; focusing primary attention on the countries that pose the most imminent proliferation risk; and placing increased emphasis on those elements of non-proliferation strategy that go beyond efforts to try to impose it on others. It recognizes a number of limitations on the impact the United States can have on this problem, and the need for a more active role by others.

The backbone of this project was a series of case studies of the countries closest to proliferation: Pakistan, India, Israel, South Africa, Argentina and Brazil. A resumé of those studies is given in Part II of this summary report. Part I summarizes the panel's overall assessment of approaches to containing proliferation in the light of those case studies.

I. Principal findings and recommendations

General conclusions

1. *Containing the spread of nuclear weapons to additional countries is of signal importance to national, regional and global security and stability, and is becoming increasingly difficult and urgent.* Further proliferation of nuclear weapons would magnify the potential destructiveness of regional hostilities, increase the risk of superpower involvement in a nuclear war, greatly complicate defense planning, create new obstacles to nuclear arms control, and enlarge the risk that nuclear weapons would come into the hands of subnational or terrorist groups. It would be extremely unlikely to result in stable mutual nuclear deterrence between regional antagonists.

   Yet, as noted above, more states are acquiring the capabilities needed to make nuclear weapons, and several of them appear bent on doing so; technical barriers are diminishing; potential sources of the necessary ingredients are multiplying; and the current broad international consensus against further proliferation is facing new challenges.

2. *The near-term risk is from several regional antagonists and requires approaches tailored to their particular circumstances, including greater efforts to reduce underlying regional tensions and to gain their recognition of the limited utility of nuclear weapons and the relative advantage of mutual abstinence from them.*

   These cases are surveyed in Part II below.

3. *Both to help deal with these cases and to prevent even more destabilizing developments, it is also essential to preserve and extend*

   - *the international consensus against proliferation that now exists among most states capable of acquiring nuclear weapons or helping others to do so,* and

   - *the international commitments reflecting and reenforcing that consensus.*

   These commitments, which include the Non-Proliferation Treaty (Appendix B), the Treaty of Tlatelolco (for the prohibition of nuclear weapons in Latin America), the safeguards agreements of the International Atomic Energy Agency; the Limited Test Ban Treaty, and the Nuclear Suppliers' Guidelines (Appendixes D and E), are discussed in paragraphs 17–22 below.

4. *The use of export controls to restrict the capabilities of non-nuclear-weapon states to make nuclear explosives can help in some cases, but has significant limitations that justify some distinctions in treatment.*

In addition to strict export controls on equipment and components directly usable in nuclear weapons manufacture, restraint should continue to be exercised in the export of weapons-usable materials (highly enriched uranium or separated plutonium) or facilities for their production (enrichment or reprocessing facilities and related technology and components), especially where the potential recipient:

—has no convincing present need for such items in its civil nuclear program;

—has not made credible, comprehensive non-proliferation commitments and accepted safeguards on all its nuclear activities;

—is located in a volatile region; or

—poses other special risks of proliferation or of subnational or terrorist intervention.

The main reason for such restraint is that for most countries, access to sufficient weapons-usable material is the pacing item in acquiring the capability to make nuclear explosives. Such restraint can also help limit the targets of opportunity for the theft or seizure of weapons-usable material.

But the following limitations on this approach should be recognized:

—For some advanced industrial countries (such as the Federal Republic of Germany, Japan, and Canada) the bulwark against proliferation is not a lack of weapons-usable materials or other capabilities needed to make nuclear weapons, since they already have all the essential materials and capabilities, but their decision that acquiring nuclear explosives would not be in their interest and the international commitments that reflect and reenforce that decision.

—Although attempts to deny the acquisition of the requisite capabilities by other states may impede, delay, or limit the extent of such acquisition and buy time for dissuasion, they cannot, in most cases, prevent a sufficiently determined state from eventually acquiring them.

—Excessive restrictions on nuclear exports can undermine support for non-proliferation efforts by countries whose cooperation is essential or, where the affected country has avoided non-proliferation commitments, stimulate its acquisition of indigenous capabilities free of any international controls.

5. *While primary emphasis must continue to be placed on averting the acquisition of a first nuclear device, the containment of proliferation also includes the need to head off subsequent steps, such as:*

- *testing, weaponization, production and deployment of such devices or of more advanced types of nuclear weapons;**

- *assistance to other states in acquiring nuclear weapons; and*

- *use or threat of use of such weapons.*

This can be even more difficult to achieve than preventing acquisition of the first bomb, but it is not necessarily impossible. (There appears to have been a suspension of Indian work on nuclear explosives following its initial explosion in 1974.) Responses to proliferatory acts should be designed to head off such further steps, as well as to deter others from crossing the first threshold.

6. *Special precautions are also needed against the separate risk of theft or seizure of nuclear weapons or sensitive material or facilities by subnational or international terrorist groups for blackmail or blackmarket purposes.* These precautions include:

—minimizing the targets of opportunity;

—employing mechanisms that render such items useless to unauthorized persons;

—providing fuller international exchanges of information on potential threats; and

---

* E.g., Israel and South Africa appear to see some advantage in maintaining uncertainty about whether they have produced nuclear weapons. Testing would dispel this ambiguity and could stimulate nuclear weapons acquisition by adversaries and damage their relations with countries important to their needs. While a first test, such as India's, can demonstrate a capability to make nuclear explosives, adapting this knowledge to usable weapons requires additional costly effort that may include further tests, as would the development of more advanced explosive designs. Factors affecting the decision to produce a stockpile of nuclear weapons include satisfaction that the weapons designs already developed by the country concerned are adequate for the purpose, that sufficient weapons-usable materials and other essential ingredients are available, and that stockpiling such weapons would enhance deterrence or war-fighting capabilities and would not be counterproductive. Decisions to deploy nuclear weapons require further military, political, and strategic judgements.

—enhancing the physical protection of items at risk, including wider adherence to the International Convention on the Physical Protection of Nuclear Material (Appendix F) that deals with problems of international transport, recovery and return of stolen materials, and establishment of criminal penalties and other enforcement mechanisms.

Containing the near-term risks

7. *Central to any strategy to contain proliferation should be intensified efforts to reduce underlying tensions between potential nuclear antagonists.* The risk of Pakistan's acquiring nuclear weapons would be reduced by improvement in its relations with India; the risk of resumption of the Indian explosive program, by improved Indian relations with Pakistan and China; the risk of further Israeli proliferation, by progress toward a Middle East peace settlement; the South African risk, by progress in reducing tensions with bordering states and territories; and the Argentinian and Brazilian risks, by closer ties between them. Where possible, mutual abstinence from nuclear weapons should be made an element of these peace-making efforts.

This point illustrates the limitations of attempting to deal with non-proliferation in isolation, and the need to recognize the relevance of broader aspects of foreign policy.

8. *A government considering the acquisition of nuclear explosives should be encouraged—preferably by other non-nuclear states—to give due weight to such questions as the following:*

—Would not its acquisition of nuclear explosives reduce its security by stimulating the acquisition of nuclear weapons by its adversaries, impairing existing security relationships with its allies, or causing increased backing of its adversaries by a nuclear weapon state?

—Are nuclear weapons relevant to the particular security threats it faces? (E.g., it is difficult to see their relevance to the principal threats facing South Africa, or the need for nuclear deterrence by Argentina or Brazil if their mutual abstinence from nuclear explosives could be achieved.)

—Are there not severe constraints on the actual use of nuclear weapons posed by the high risk of retaliation and escalation and (in the case of use in friendly territory) of collateral damage to friendly populations and forces?

—Is there not a greater improbability of maintaining a stable mutual deterrence between regional antagonists than between the super-powers? (Differences include the multiplicity of actors, their acute hostility, greater volatility, vulnerability, command and control problems, and the special risks involved before they could achieve a survivable second-strike capability.)

—Would not mutual abstinence from nuclear weapons provide greater assurance against their use than mutual nuclear deterrence?

—Is it prepared to become embroiled in an open-ended nuclear arms race, with constant pressure for more advanced weapons and delivery systems, and a consequent drain on resources available for conventional military preparedness and other purposes?

—Is its policy toward "peaceful nuclear explosions" realistic, given the lack of any serious near-term prospects for practical, environmentally acceptable peaceful applications of such explosions; the fact that most such applications would require thermonuclear devices that could not be developed without a very extensive and costly program and many test explosions; and the security advantage of averting the development of nuclear explosives under this guise by a rival state?

—Is it prepared to run the risk of preemptive attacks on the nuclear facilities involved in its weapons program?

—Is it prepared to face the substantial setbacks to its nuclear power program that would result from being cut off from necessary imports? (This consideration obviously has greatest weight in countries where nuclear power constitutes a significant portion of electric power supply.)

—Is it prepared to risk being denied other types of international cooperation that might be withheld if it acquired nuclear weapons?

Clearly, the burden of persuasion will be greater in the case of a non-nuclear weapon state whose regional rival already has some nuclear weapons, but even here there may well be an interest in keeping the rival from enlarging that advantage.

9. *Comprehensive safeguards coverage in non-nuclear weapon states should continue to be vigorously sought, with further efforts to persuade suppliers to make such coverage a condition of any significant new commitments.* In each of the six cases of greatest near-term proliferation concern, unsafeguarded facilities are the principal focus of concern. If these facilities were under safeguards, their operation and the disposition of their output could be closely monitored, and

the safeguards agreement would include a commitment not to divert them to explosive use or to export their output without safeguards. Yet in most of these countries the resistance to comprehensive safeguards coverage is high, and unlikely to be overcome by adding minor items to the list of exports to be denied to non-nuclear weapon states unwilling to accept such comprehensive safeguards.

10. *A comprehensive test ban treaty could make a significant contribution to containing proliferation.* Such a treaty has been persistently advocated by most of the non-nuclear weapon states of greatest concern (including a 1985 declaration joined by the new leaders of India and Argentina), though it is not clear that all of them would actually join it. For non-nuclear weapon states other than India, abstinence from testing would mean that they could not demonstrate the achievement of a nuclear explosive capability or have full confidence that they had achieved it; and for all non-nuclear weapon states it would effectively preclude the development of improved or advanced types of explosives, such as miniaturized, boosted, or thermonuclear weapons, and the explosives needed for most purported "peaceful" applications. Moreover, the achievement of such a treaty, even if not joined by all the non-nuclear weapon states of greatest concern, would help preserve the viability of the Non-Proliferation Treaty by providing the most widely demanded response to the complaint that the superpowers are not meeting their obligations under that Treaty to pursue nuclear arms control.

Well over two-thirds of the U.S. Senate passed a resolution in 1984 calling for the resumption of negotiations on such a treaty, as well as for resubmission to the Senate of the unratified Threshold Test Ban Treaty; and a similar 1985 resolution in the House of Representatives has more than 200 co-sponsors. The vast majority of NPT parties attending the 1985 Review Conference identified a comprehensive test ban as the top priority among nuclear arms control measures, and this view was reflected in the Final Declaration of that Conference.

11. *Substantial strengthening of existing security commitments from the nuclear-weapon states to the states of greatest near-term concern does not appear politically feasible.* None of the nuclear-weapon states has or is likely to make such commitments to South Africa. Israel's unique informal security relationship with the United States goes beyond any formal commitment it could be given, and a formal commitment would increase the difficulty of

working with other Middle Eastern countries towards a Middle East peace settlement. Pakistan has a mutual security agreement and strategic relationship with the United States, reaffirmed in 1981,* and India a Treaty of Friendship and Cooperation with the Soviet Union, but positive security commitments specifically related to the threat these two South Asian countries pose to each other are not in the cards. Argentina and Brazil are parties to the Rio Treaty and do not currently face military threats from each other.

12. *"Negative" security assurances to most of these states are unpromising, with the possible exception of a Soviet agreement with Pakistan on this subject.* The only existing treaty commitments by the nuclear weapon states not to use or threaten to use nuclear weapons against specified countries are those in Additional Protocol II to the Treaty for the Prohibition of Nuclear Weapons in Latin America (the Treaty of Tlatelolco). Argentina and Brazil could automatically obtain their benefit by becoming full parties to that treaty, though they face no plausible nuclear threats from any nuclear weapon state. The Soviet Union has frequently declared that it would also be prepared to enter into bilateral agreements extending such "negative" security assurances to any state that agreed not to acquire nuclear weapons or have them stationed on its territory. While the latter condition is obviously unacceptable with respect to most U.S. allies, such a Soviet agreement with Pakistan might be possible and acceptable, since the Pakistanis have long professed interest in obtaining negative security assurances; they face a potential Soviet threat on which they may consider it useful to place some inhibition (however fragile); it is virtually inconceivable that the United States would wish to station nuclear weapons in Pakistan; and the case is clearly distinguishable from those of our European and East Asian allies.†

"Negative" security assurances from the United States do not appear relevant to the security threats faced by Israel, South Africa, India, or Pakistan. South Korea would be likely to view such assurances to North Korea as undercutting deterrence of the principal threat it faces. India generally considers such assurances illusory. The Soviet Union cannot be expected to extend them to Israel or South Africa.

---

* The question of extending U.S. economic and military assistance to Pakistan beyond FY 1987 is addressed in paragraph 14 below.

† Some members of the panel thought the risk that some of these other allies might be tempted to seek such an agreement outweighed any advantages that might be gained in this case.

13. *The leverage available to help contain proliferation is highly case-specific and, though it may be useful in some cases, its limitations should be recognized.* For example, the leverage provided by interest in international nuclear cooperation—while substantial in cases such as Taiwan and the Republic of Korea—is extremely modest in most of the cases of current concern (such as Pakistan, Israel, South Africa, and India). Although the serious international debt problems of Argentina and Brazil might at first blush appear to offer potential leverage, the actual withholding of debt relief from such countries would be counterproductive, undermine their promising new civilian regimes, and hurt the creditor countries at least as much as the debtors. (This, of course, does not preclude highlighting the fact that proliferatory actions would add to the difficulties of arranging for debt relief.) Our examination of the possibilities of pressure through the multilateral aid organizations likewise disclosed some limitations in most of the cases of concern.

14. *Present U.S. non-proliferation legislation has little impact on most states of near-term concern, but with a few possible exceptions, its amendment or repeal would not be particularly helpful.* The principal leverage of the Nuclear Non-Proliferation Act of 1978 is the threat to cut off U.S. nuclear cooperation, but (partly as a result of that Act) we no longer have any significant nuclear cooperation with any of the six countries of greatest near-term concern. Thus, we cannot use this leverage to deter or respond to further proliferatory steps by these countries. Likewise, the leverage of the non-proliferation provisions of the U.S. Foreign Assistance Act is suspension of economic assistance and military credits and grants, but of the six countries of greatest concern, the only two to which we provide any significant economic or military assistance are Pakistan (where the cut-off threat still has some utility) and Israel (where a cut-off would be subject to serious U.S. domestic political constraints). These provisions could, however, affect Taiwan or South Korea if they were to resume proliferatory activities.

Repeal or amendment of the existing legislation would create further confusion and intensify the impression that U.S. policy in this field was too changeable to constitute a basis for a long-term supply relationship. Neither repeal nor amendments designed to *loosen* existing restrictions appear politically achievable at this time, and even if achieved might eliminate some useful reforms without significantly enhancing U.S. nuclear commerce. Amendments designed to *tighten* existing restrictions could further exacerbate our relationship with our principal trading partners (whose cooperation is needed for an effective non-proliferation regime) without significantly decreasing the risk of further proliferation. (For example, this would be the most likely effect of amendments attempting to deny access to weapons-usable materials to all non-nuclear weapon states, regardless of their circumstances.)

One helpful 1985 amendment to the Foreign Assistance Act was that which requires a cut-off of military and economic grants and credits to a country that illegally imports from the United States material, equipment, or technology that would contribute significantly to its ability to manufacture a nuclear explosive device if the President determines it was to be used for that purpose. (While this amendment was in response to Pakistan's illegal procurement of U.S. krytrons, apparently for use as nuclear triggers, Israel also imported some U.S. krytrons without a U.S. export license.)

Another possible exception is the provision of the Foreign Assistance Act authorizing economic and military assistance to Pakistan, which expires September 30, 1987, unless earlier terminated by a Pakistan nuclear detonation or by a transfer of nuclear weapons by Pakistan to another state. Depending on the situation in Afghanistan and the status of South Asian proliferation, it will be necessary to consider whether or not to introduce an amendment authorizing a follow-on package of assistance to Pakistan, and what non-proliferation conditions and assurances should be required in that connection.

15. *The U.S. government should declare and encourage other governments to declare that violation of international non-proliferation commitments, or detonation of a nuclear explosive by a non-nuclear weapon state, would meet with severe adverse responses not necessarily limited to suspension of international nuclear cooperation.* Advance agreement on specific concerted multinational responses to such events is probably unattainable in view of the reluctance of governments to commit themselves to particular courses of action before knowing the identity of the parties or the exact circumstances involved. There is also some disadvantage in being too specific about the nature of the threatened response, since that would make it easier for a violator to design around it.

The reason this recommendation deals only with violations and nuclear detonations is the difficulty of obtaining international consensus that, where no violation of an international undertaking is involved, sanctions should be applied to an activity such as the acquisition of weapons-usable materials or facilities from which they could be recovered. But this need not preclude the use in a particularly sensitive case (such as Pakistan) of available leverage to dissuade a country from taking further steps towards attaining the capability to make nuclear weapons.

16. *If a violation or detonation does occur, prompt resort should be made to the consultative and coordinating mechanisms provided for in the Nuclear Suppliers' Guidelines.* These mechanisms (paragraph 14c of Appendix D) are designed to facilitate a coordinated international response and to avoid the risk that a response made by one supplier country will be undercut by actions of another. They can also help build the consensus needed to apply the sanctions contemplated by the Statute of the International Atomic Energy Agency (cut-off of nuclear cooperation and referral to the United Nations Security Council.)

A failure to respond to a violation or detonation would make the perpetrator less hesitant to proceed further up the proliferation ladder and reduce the deterrence of similar actions by other states.

Preserving and extending the international non-proliferation regime

17. *High priority should be given to laying the groundwork for extending the Non-Proliferation Treaty beyond 1995.* At the NPT Review Conference in 1990—which could well be contentious—it will be important to focus attention on the positive contributions of the Treaty and to avoid outcomes threatening its continued viability. To extend the Treaty beyond 1995, a majority vote of the parties will be required—which should not be taken for granted in view of the mounting criticism of the lack of progress in achieving nuclear arms control. If the Treaty were allowed to expire, the glue that holds the non-proliferation regime together would cease to hold; its parties would lose the benefit of reciprocal treaty obligations; and the related safeguards agreements would expire. It is none too early to begin work on a strategy to avoid an impasse in 1995.

Such a strategy—building on the success of the 1985 NPT Review Conference (Appendix C)—should emphasize above all the security value of the NPT and IAEA safeguards to its parties. But it should also include maintenance of confidence in existing security arrangements and efforts of the type suggested in this report to head off further actual proliferation crises; enhanced support for the IAEA and its safeguards system; actions to buttress the case that adherence to the NPT facilitates the enjoyment of peaceful international nuclear cooperation; and greater sensitivity by the nuclear weapon states to the impact of what they do and say about their own nuclear weapons, preferably including demonstrable arms control achievements.

18. *In Latin America, the Treaty of Tlatelolco remains the most promising vehicle for containing proliferation. Argentine ratification of that Treaty—and of the Limited Test Ban Treaty—should be sought as soon as politically feasible.* Tactics on this matter must take account of the other formidable political problems faced by the Alfonsin regime and the desirability, both for non-proliferation and other reasons, of its remaining in office. Completion of French ratification of Additional Protocol I to the Treaty (subjecting to the Treaty French territories located in Latin America) should also be pursued, and the Soviets should be encouraged to press harder for Cuban adherence to the Treaty. These steps would help bring the Treaty into force for Brazil, which ratified it subject to the precondition that these further adherences take place.

19. *Meanwhile, constructive steps such as the following should be encouraged:*

(a) *development and implementation of arrangements by Argentina and Brazil for mutual inspection of all of each other's nuclear facilities.* An agreement in principle to negotiate such arrangements was reached by President Alfonsin and President-elect Neves before his untimely death, and the present leaders of the two countries have recently initiated such negotiations. (With respect to the similar offer by Pakistan to India to negotiate such arrangements, the deep suspicions underlying Indo-Pakistani relations and the large lead held by India's nuclear program over Pakistan's make achievement of such an agreement between the two countries implausible.)

(b) *an exchange of assurances by Argentina and Brazil that neither has any actual current plans to develop nuclear explosives for "peaceful" purposes, and that each would consult the other and the IAEA before initiating such development.* This approach would avoid the need to renounce the theoretical legal right to develop nuclear explosives for "peaceful" purposes while providing mutual assurance that this "right" would not be exercised without prior consultation. This could help break the current impasse with the IAEA over the terms of the Argentine safeguards agreement under the Treaty of Tlatelolco. (As indicated below, the possibility of a similar exchange between India and Pakistan seems worth exploring.)

20. *More widespread application of the export policies prescribed by the Nuclear Suppliers' Guidelines should be sought.* The Guidelines were adopted in 1977 by the fifteen principal nuclear supplier countries.* They establish common standards for safeguards and other conditions of nuclear supply, and call for restraint in the export of particularly sensitive nuclear materials and facilities. Nine other states† have since declared that their export policies conform with the Guidelines. Another promising candidate for adherence is Spain, a potentially significant exporter that joined Euratom in January 1986. Subscribers to the Guidelines constitute one of the most promising groups for consultations on proliferation crises and on further improvements in nuclear export controls. Special efforts should be made to persuade

—India and other significant non-subscribers to adopt comparable policies; and

—newly emerging suppliers such as Argentina and China not to undercut the consensus established by the Guidelines.‡

21. *The United States should give full, uninterrupted political, technical and financial support to the International Atomic Energy Agency and its safeguards system.* The IAEA is of unique value to the United States and to the implementation of non-proliferation policy. It has the principal responsibility for monitoring compliance with the Non-Proliferation Treaty, the Treaty of Tlatelolco, and virtually all of the world's agreements for international nuclear commerce. In 1982–83, the United States temporarily suspended its participation in the IAEA and held up payment of its assessed and pledged contributions in protest against attempts to curtail the membership rights of Israel. In the event of any comparable provocations in the future, this response should be avoided and the United States should find other means to register its disagreement that do not jeopardize the international safeguards system. Likewise, Congress should support uninterrupted funding of the IAEA and avoid passing legislation that could impair that goal.

* The United States, France, the Federal Republic of Germany, the Soviet Union, the United Kingdom, Canada, Japan, Belgium, Czechoslovakia, the German Democratic Republic, Italy, The Netherlands, Poland, Sweden, and Switzerland.

† Australia, Bulgaria, Denmark, Finland, Greece, Hungary, Ireland, Luxembourg, and South Africa.

‡ Both have at least declared that they would require IAEA safeguards on their nuclear exports. For observations on the recent U.S.-China Agreement for Cooperation, see Appendix H.

22. *What the nuclear weapon states do and say about their own nuclear weapons, and about nuclear arms control, will probably affect the long-term prospects for containing proliferation.* For the states of greatest near-term concern, these factors may well not be decisive in their assessment of the costs and benefits of forswearing nuclear weapons. But increasing emphasis by the nuclear weapon states on the military utility of nuclear weapons, and continued lack of progress—or, worse yet, retrogression—in nuclear arms control, would heighten resentment by the non-nuclear weapon states of the double standard and affect the legitimacy of the non-proliferation regime. Moreover, within the problem states, such developments would strengthen the hand of those favoring proliferation and also create serious obstacles to extending the Non-Proliferation Treaty beyond 1995.

Role of others

23. *To contain proliferation, countries other than the United States must play an increased role:*

- *In nuclear export controls:* The growing share of the weakened nuclear export market held by other countries (such as France, the Federal Republic of Germany, Canada, Japan, and the Soviet Union) increases the need for their cooperation in nuclear export controls. The emergence of new sources of supply (such as China, Spain, India, and Argentina) creates a need to make sure that they will not undercut such measures;

- *In persuading others not to acquire nuclear explosives:* Non-nuclear states are likely to be more persuasive than the nuclear weapons states, which are advocating a position they have not accepted for themselves;

- *In coordinating responses to actual or imminent proliferation crises:* Nations other than the United States can provide significant leverage, sometimes of kinds we do not have.

They can also:

- *Help maintain the international non-proliferation regime:* Broad support is necessary for its survival; and

- *Encourage nuclear-weapon-free zones in other suitable regions of the world:* Visible U.S. pressure for such zones is likely to be counterproductive (though once any such zone is created, U.S. support for it will be sought and should be seriously considered).

24. *Efforts should be made to stimulate support for non-proliferation by influential non-government individuals and groups within countries of concern as well as by friendly states.* Opportunities for this approach differ widely between countries. Brazil and Argentina present new opportunities for domestic debate and may be susceptible to some influence by other Latin American countries such as Mexico and Venezuela, or by the West Germans. In India the debate goes on as to whether the country would gain or suffer by acquiring nuclear weapons. The weight of public opinion tends to be nationalistic and "pro-bomb"; spokesmen for the minority seek and merit encouragement. There are some limited opportunities (without much chance of having a decisive influence) for domestic debate on this issue in Israel and South Africa.

25. *Fuller development and integration of West European non-proliferation policy should be pursued.* This is a major focus of the accompanying study by a separate West European panel. While gratifying recent progress has been made on this score, use of the European Communities as an integrating mechanism should be further encouraged. The new membership of Spain and Portugal will present important opportunities in this respect.

26. *Continued cooperation with the Soviet Union on non-proliferation is necessary and desirable.* As indicated by the joint statement issued at the November 1985 Geneva Summit (Appendix G), the United States and the Soviet Union share a strong common interest in preventing further proliferation. Soviet cooperation is needed to ensure:

—common nuclear export policies;

—support of international non-proliferation efforts by Soviet allies and clients (including Cuba); and

—progress in meeting demands to curb the nuclear arms race.

Even at times when relations between our two countries have otherwise been under the greatest strain, the Soviets have remained staunch supporters of the non-proliferation regime, generally cautious in their nuclear export policy, and willing to consult on pending proliferation problems.

These consultations are useful despite some differences on particular cases and the risk of arousing charges of hegemony or condominium. Collaboration on this subject can also keep open the door for constructive U.S.-Soviet dialogue on other subjects—especially on nuclear arms control which, as noted above, will affect the long-run prospects for containing proliferation.

II. The countries of greatest near-term proliferation concern

An overview of the results of the panel's case studies of *Pakistan, India, Israel, South Africa, Argentina,* and *Brazil* is given below, together with brief observations on several other countries of concern.

None of the six countries named above is a party to the Non-Proliferation Treaty or likely to become one in the near future; none has accepted full-scope safeguards; and each has, or is building, one or more unsafeguarded facilities capable of producing weapons-usable material. All but two of them are parties to the Limited Test Ban Treaty, while the other two (Argentina and Pakistan) have signed but not ratified it, which they should be pressed to do. None of them currently has significant nuclear cooperation with the United States. And neither Argentina nor Brazil is yet fully bound by the Treaty of Tlatelolco.*

In addition to these holdouts, there has been particular concern about a few states that have officially joined the Non-Proliferation Treaty. Of these, the risk of proliferation seems to have subsided in *Taiwan* and *South Korea* but could, in some circumstances, reappear.† *Libya*—however sinister Col. Qaddafi's aspirations—is still far from achieving the capabilities to make nuclear explosives, has its nuclear activities under close Soviet scrutiny as well as IAEA safeguards, and seems unlikely to persuade any nuclear weapon state to sell it a nuclear weapon (but might succeed in obtaining some weapons-usable material or, conceivably, in seizing or stealing a weapon). *Iran's* nuclear program and infrastructure have been sharply curtailed by the revolutionary government, especially during the war with Iraq, though they may be revived and could well become a source of special concern in the medium term, given the extreme militancy of its present government, its growing affiliation with Syria and Libya, and its hostility toward Iraq. Likewise, despite the substantial set-back in its capabilities caused by the destruction of its large research reactor, *Iraq* could become a renewed source of concern in the medium term.

---

* Brazil has ratified it, but not waived certain preconditions for its application to Brazil, including Argentine ratification. Argentina has signed but not yet ratified it.

† The reported construction by North Korea of an unsafeguarded research reactor is a new cause of concern, though mitigated by its joining the NPT in December 1985.

Pakistan

The most pressing current case is Pakistan, which appears to be proceeding towards the development of a nuclear weapons capability. It has been building unsafeguarded uranium enrichment and chemical reprocessing facilities (bearing no reasonable relationship to its civil nuclear program) with which it could produce highly enriched uranium or separated plutonium needed to make nuclear weapons; and it has engaged in a number of other activities indicative of a nuclear weapons program, reportedly including test-site preparations, relevant high-explosive experimentation, clandestine attempts to import non-nuclear items used in nuclear weapons, and alleged receipt of pertinent information from the Chinese. It appears to have refrained, however, from helping others to acquire the capabilities to make nuclear weapons and has repeatedly denied any intentions of producing such weapons itself.

Concerted international efforts to impede and delay the completion of the unsafeguarded Pakistani enrichment and reprocessing facilities have helped slow it down, but Pakistan may already have succeeded in obtaining some weapons-usable material and, unless dissuaded, would be capable of producing enough such material in the near future to make a few nuclear weapons. These international efforts, though not by themselves sufficient, should be continued. Pakistan's recent announcement that it would confine the operation of its enrichment facilities to the production of low-enriched uranium should be welcomed and reflected in approaches to Pakistan. While it has offered to negotiate mutual inspection arrangements with the Indians, the latter seem unlikely to engage in such negotiations.

The most helpful approaches to containing the proliferation risk in this region would be (a) encouraging intensified efforts by India and Pakistan to reduce the underlying tensions between them and (b) convincing Pakistan that its acquisition of nuclear explosives would not be in its best interest, and that it has more to gain from arrangements with India for mutual abstinence that could head off resumption of the Indian nuclear explosive program.

A significant disincentive to Pakistan's conducting a nuclear weapons test (or to its transferring a nuclear explosive device to another non-nuclear weapon state) in the next two years is its interest in avoiding the loss of the current $3.2 billion U.S. economic and military assistance package, and its security backing by the

United States. The package, spread over 5 years (ending September 30, 1987), is about evenly divided between economic assistance and military credits, and includes a sale of 40 F-16s, of which some remain to be delivered and all require continued servicing and spare parts. It was made possible by a 1981 Foreign Assistance Act amendment that also included a provision for terminating such assistance to any non-nuclear weapon state that thereafter detonated a nuclear explosive device or transferred such a device to another non-nuclear weapon state, and declared that such actions would cause "grave damage" to our bilateral relations. The extension of such a package beyond FY 1987 will of course depend on the status of the Soviet occupation of Afghanistan and of the Pakistani nuclear program. But if there have not been significant changes, consideration should be given to a follow-on package conditioned on tighter assurances against Pakistan's proceeding further towards a nuclear weapons capability (including, for example, avoidance of unsafeguarded reprocessing, and reassurance that it will not produce highly enriched uranium and that it will adhere strictly to safeguards obligations), coupled with serious efforts to ensure that these conditions are not undercut by others.

Other current disincentives to a Pakistani nuclear weapons test include Pakistan's recognition of the likelihood that a test would precipitate resumption of the Indian nuclear explosive program, and its uncertainty and fear of the Soviet reaction. (But note that a second Indian explosion would not only eliminate the first of these disincentives but create a further incentive.)

In addition to heading off a nuclear weapons test, it is important to avoid the severe damage to the international safeguards regime that would be done if Pakistan diverted safeguarded nuclear materials to use in a nuclear explosive—as it would probably have to do to obtain the requisite separated plutonium, since the only nuclear material known to be available to Pakistan for reprocessing is under safeguards. (Though it may have acquired some natural uranium without safeguards, it is not believed to have an unsafeguarded reactor.) In this connection, the members of the Nuclear Suppliers' Group should make clear to Pakistan that any such violation of safeguards would incur severe penalties, not limited to suspension of future nuclear cooperation.

Constructive steps that Pakistan should be urged to take include (1) ratification of the Limited Test Ban Treaty; (2) acceptance of comprehensive full-scope safeguards (which it will resist, but which should at least be made a condition of further nuclear supplies to

Pakistan by members of the Nuclear Suppliers' Group); (3) compliance with its declared dedication of its enrichment facility exclusively to the production of low-enriched uranium (which cannot be used in weapons), with corresponding monitorable restrictions on the facility's configuration and operating mode; and (4) continued caution in its nuclear export policy, so as not to become a source of further proliferation. It has offered to negotiate mutual inspection arrangements with India, though Indian receptivity is highly doubtful. But it should be encouraged to explore with India a mutual moratorium on the development of nuclear explosives for "peaceful" purposes, or at least parallel announcements that they have no current program for the development of nuclear explosives for such purposes and that before initiating (or, in the case of India, reviving) one, they would consult with each other and with the International Atomic Energy Agency.

Pakistan's interest in peaceful nuclear cooperation, while not negligible, does not provide decisive leverage. Its existing civil program is small, and though it has sought bids on a second power reactor, no bids have been received (partly because of financing problems). But so long as it appears to be pursuing a nuclear weapons program, further nuclear assistance to it should be avoided by all foreign suppliers, including China.

Extension of security assurances to Pakistan beyond those in our mutual security agreement of 1959 (which was reaffirmed in 1981) does not seem politically feasible, but the value that Pakistanis may place on our growing *de facto* security relationship should not be underestimated. Pakistan has long expressed interest in "negative" security assurances from the nuclear weapon states—i.e., treaty commitments or other assurances that they will not use or threaten to use nuclear weapons against Pakistan. The only states that pose potential nuclear threats to Pakistan are the Soviet Union and India. The former has indicated that it would be prepared to enter into bilateral non-use agreements with non-nuclear-weapon states that have not acquired nuclear weapons and do not have them stationed on their territory, and such an agreement might be possible. While Pakistan could meet these conditions and has not dismissed non-use assurances as illusory, it would be necessary to distinguish this special case from those of U.S. allies on whose territory we do station, or may contemplate stationing, nuclear weapons. The theoretical possibility of mutual "non-use" assurances between India and Pakistan is probably a non-starter in view of strong indications that Indian officials consider such assurances illusory, but it might nevertheless be raised in the context of efforts to improve relations between the two countries.

Pakistan's attempts to interest India in a South Asian nuclear-weapons-free zone have been regularly rejected by India, which insists that China would have to be included in any such zone, and that seems clearly unattainable at this time.

Pakistan has generally supported U.N. resolutions urging the conclusion of a comprehensive test ban, as has India. If such a treaty were concluded, it is quite conceivable that these two countries would join it. If they did so, it would provide India with a commitment precluding Pakistani demonstration of a nuclear explosive capability and development of more advanced explosives, and provide Pakistan with a commitment precluding resumption of the Indian test program or Indian development of more advanced nuclear explosives.

India

India has a demonstrated capability to make nuclear weapons, and its inventories of weapons-usable materials free of international commitments are growing. But after its 1974 test explosion it appears to have suspended its nuclear weapons program (although some research short of a nuclear test explosion may well have continued), and it has avoided helping other states to acquire the capabilities to make such explosives. Thus, the most immediate non-proliferation objectives with respect to India are to head off the resumption of its nuclear explosive program and to persuade it to continue its cautious nuclear export policy. The broader challenge of persuading India that the acquisition of nuclear explosives would not be in its net interest depends in part upon heading off the acquisition of nuclear weapons by Pakistan (including further Chinese assistance) and in part upon improvements in the relations of India with Pakistan and China. India's new Prime Minister, Rajiv Gandhi, has indicated his intention to seek such improvements.

Many of the approaches suggested above for dealing with Pakistan are less promising for India. It is too late to avoid Indian access to enough unsafeguarded weapons-usable material for a small nuclear weapons program, but suppliers should continue to avoid exports likely to increase such access. India will almost certainly not accept full-scope safeguards. Although India is more nearly self-sufficient in this field than Pakistan and is continuing to strengthen its nuclear industrial base, its stake in nuclear power is higher. Its relative independence in this field is being bought at the price of substantial delays, inefficiencies, and other setbacks in its own nuclear power program and of losing the benefit of foreign improvements in the state of the art. India does not appear to be as close as Pakistan to having an operative uranium enrichment plant. If one were to be built, India should be urged to dedicate it to low enrichment only and to place it under international safeguards. India's lack of interest in negative security assurances and in a South Asian nuclear-weapon-free zone have already been noted, as has the political infeasibility of stronger positive security assurances against Pakistan, over whom India enjoys considerable conventional military superiority.

Bilateral U.S. economic and military assistance to India is too small to provide significant leverage. However, the aggregate of all economic and military assistance provided to India by members of the Nuclear Suppliers' Group is significant enough to provide a potential multilateral disincentive to further proliferatory acts, though clearly insufficient if India should decide its national security required nuclear weapons.

Despite the deep antipathies that persist and the frustrations experienced in the past, further efforts to reduce the underlying tensions between India and Pakistan and between India and China are basic to an effective non-proliferation strategy. Another promising approach would be a comprehensive test ban treaty, if other obstacles to its achievement could be overcome. (As noted above, Prime Minister Rajiv Gandhi recently joined with Argentine President Alfonsin and others in a plea for such a treaty.) And some form of mutual Indo-Pakistani moratorium on programs for the development of nuclear explosives for "peaceful" purposes should be explored. Mutual inspection arrangements appear to have little chance of being negotiable with India.

Israel and the Middle East

Of all the states other than the five acknowledged nuclear weapon states, Israel is the one where development of the capacity to make nuclear weapons has proceeded the furthest, where interest in preventing further proliferation by others is the strongest, and where the relevance of peace-making efforts to containing proliferation risks is the most obvious. It is also the case in which the United States would appear to have the greatest leverage, but where the use of such leverage is most severely constrained by domestic political considerations and some degree of ambivalence. It could prove to be the Achilles heel of our non-proliferation policy.

Although it has not yet begun to build or contracted to acquire a nuclear power plant, Israel is by far the most advanced state in the Middle East in nuclear technology. Experts agree that it either has a number of untested nuclear weapons or could produce them on very short notice. It almost certainly has enough unsafeguarded weapons-usable material to have produced such weapons. The unsafeguarded Dimona reactor has been operating for many years and is likely to have produced enough plutonium for a significant number of weapons; Israel has obtained enough unsafeguarded uranium to fuel that reactor and has access to enough heavy water to operate it; and it has an unsafeguarded pilot reprocessing facility at Dimona in which it has separated plutonium. (It is also possible that some highly enriched uranium missing from a plant at Apollo, Pennsylvania, ended up in Israel). The Israelis have an unusually high level of nuclear expertise and are generally presumed to be capable of manufacturing nuclear warheads. Moreover, Israel has advanced aircraft and missiles that could be used to deliver nuclear weapons at least against nearby targets.

Thus, the capabilities to make and deliver nuclear weapons are clearly present, and (though a party to the Limited Test Ban Treaty) Israel has avoided any international commitment not to acquire such weapons, other than its repeated declaration that it will not be the first to introduce nuclear weapons into the Middle East.

The other states in the region are far behind in acquiring the requisite capabilities, and (except for Pakistan) those that have any significant nuclear programs (Iraq, Iran, Libya, and Egypt) are parties to the Limited Test Ban Treaty and the Non-Proliferation Treaty and have accepted full-scope safeguards. As noted above, the Iranian and Iraqi programs have suffered serious setbacks, and the Libyan program is proceeding slowly and under close Soviet scrutiny. Egypt, which has made peace with Israel, hopes to acquire its first power reactors (which will not be completed before the early 1990s) and has a long-term contract with the United States to supply low-enriched uranium for them. Its agreement for cooperation with the United States precludes the reprocessing or storage in Egypt of the spent fuel produced in reactors in which U.S. fuel is used, or the storage of the separated plutonium in Egypt.

The Israeli situation described above has now existed for some years. A minimal U.S. objective is to keep it from getting worse and to head off further steps by Israel (such as nuclear explosive testing; adoption of an overt nuclear deterrent posture; future production, stockpiling, or deployment of nuclear weapons; or development and exploitation of more advanced types of nuclear weapons) that would intensify the pressure on its neighbors to acquire their own nuclear weapons or at least to seek nuclear guarantees from the Soviet Union. Above all, U.S. policy should seek to avert the actual use of nuclear weapons in the Middle East.

It is difficult to deny that the presumption that Israel has nuclear weapons has some deterrent value under current circumstances, where no other state in the region yet possesses such weapons. This would not be enhanced by an Israeli nuclear detonation, which would be detrimental to its relationship with the United States and stimulate nuclear explosive programs by its adversaries. In the long run, the best insurance against nuclear war in the region would be mutual abstinence from the possession of nuclear weapons, if still achievable, since the prospects for a stable mutual deterrence after one or more of Israel's adversaries acquired nuclear weapons would be dim.

There is a substantial question whether heading off further pro-liferatory steps by Israel would be enough to prevent the abandon-ment of non-proliferation commitments by those Arab states that have made them, and whether, or how soon, the Israeli capability will be countered by the acquisition of relevant capabilities or even nuclear weapons by one or more of its antagonists. While these out-comes may still be some years away, it would seem worse for Israel's security than if Israel relied on its conventional military superiority, and seriously pursued agreements for mutual abstinence from nu-clear weapons.

That Israel is acutely conscious of the need to prevent the acquisition of nuclear weapons by its adversaries is apparent from the extreme measures it took to destroy the large research reactor that Iraq had acquired from France.

It is unrealistic to expect any stronger security commitments to Israel than the unique special relationship it currently enjoys with the

United States. Israel is scornful of negative security assurances. Increasing demands for economic and military grants and credits to Israel may soon run up against U.S. budgetary limitations. But it will remain vital to Israel's survival not to jeopardize its relationship with the United States. Thus, there is ample potential leverage. The question is how willing the United States may be to use the leverage to contain Israeli proliferation.

Although Israel has for some years flirted with the idea of acquiring nuclear power reactors, it does not appear to have an overriding interest in doing so now, probably cannot afford to import them (despite reports of French-Israeli discussions of the possibility) or obtain the necessary financing, and would have great difficulty in building and fueling them indigenously without some relevant imports. The United States is effectively barred by its own legislation from providing such cooperation, seems unlikely to be willing to help finance supply by others,* and might well intervene against such supply. Thus, the risk of losing international nuclear cooperation probably constitutes little real disincentive to Israeli proliferation, but it should not receive such cooperation without accepting comprehensive, full-scope safeguards. Moreover, continued use can and should be made of export controls to try to impede and delay any new unsafeguarded Israeli nuclear activities or acquisition of non-nuclear components of nuclear weapons.

The stumbling blocks to a Middle East nuclear-weapon-free zone of the type that has been proposed by Israel include the reluctance of some Arab states to engage in direct negotiations with Israel, and the difficulty of persuading them that Israel would not in fact retain some clandestine nuclear weapons. Israeli adherence to a comprehensive test ban treaty—if one could be negotiated by the nuclear weapon states and if Israel's principal antagonists also joined it—could be a more promising approach.

South Africa

South Africa now has the capability to produce some highly enriched uranium of a grade suitable for nuclear weapons, probably could produce some first-generation weapons, and has entered into

---

* Sec. 207 of the recent Foreign Assistance Authorization Act precludes the use of U.S. economic assistance for fiscal years 1986 or 1987 to finance reactors or fuel in countries not party to the NPT or the Treaty of Tlatelolco.

no international commitment not to do so.* An apparent South African attempt to conduct an underground nuclear weapons test in 1977 was headed off by international pressures, and there has been no corroborating evidence to establish that the signals received by a U.S. satellite in the South Pacific in 1979 were caused by a South African nuclear test. But South Africa has strongly resisted accepting safeguards on its pilot enrichment plant (with which it could produce each year enough weapons-usable material for a few weapons), though declaring its readiness to accept them on a commercial enrichment facility under construction. It is also important to seek the dedication of that facility (and, if possible, the pilot plant) to the production of low-enriched uranium.

In its role as a nuclear supplier, South Africa has declared that it will follow the policy of insisting on IAEA safeguards on all its nuclear exports to non-nuclear weapon states and to act in conformity with the Nuclear Suppliers' Guidelines.

The greatest hope of containing the risk of South African proliferation (including nuclear weapons manufacture, testing, refinement, production, deployment, or use) rests on its recognizing the irrelevance of nuclear weapons to any of the actual security threats it faces. Further progress in finding a *modus vivendi* with the states and territories on its border would also be helpful, as would the availability of a comprehensive test ban treaty.

The impact of external leverage on South Africa is subject to some unique limitations. One is the relative self-sufficiency of South Africa. It neither has nor needs security commitments from other countries; it does not need or receive bilateral or multilateral economic assistance; and it is already subject to an arms embargo declared by the United Nations, to which it has responded by building up its indigenous arms industry. Where potential leverage does exist, e.g., in its foreign trade relations, there are at least two limitations on its use as a disincentive to proliferatory actions: (1) the importance to some of its trading partners of importing from South Africa certain strategic metals, and their reluctance to cut off the valuable South African market for their own exports; and (2) the multiplicity of objectives for which economic sanctions against South Africa are advocated. In the latter connection, the deterrent value of a risk of losing certain international benefits if it were to proceed with proliferatory actions is diminished by South African realization that

---

* It is, however, a party to the Limited Test Ban Treaty.

even if it refrained from such actions, it might still be deprived of such benefits for other reasons, as has become increasingly evident in recent months. But the strong South African interest in avoiding comprehensive, mandatory U.N. sanctions, and its dependence on the United States, France, and the United Kingdom to protect it against them, as well as its interest in maintaining its major political, trade, and credit relationships with the major Western countries, nevertheless provide some leverage.

In assuming no worsening of the South African proliferation problem, there is still a question as to whether concern over South African capabilities will undermine adherence to the non-proliferation regime by Nigeria and other black African countries. This could damage the regime notwithstanding the enormous technological strides they would have to make before they could actually produce a nuclear weapon and the time this would take. And it could give South Africa an excuse for openly producing nuclear weapons.

Argentina and Brazil

Argentina and Brazil now seem to us to present a less imminent risk of proliferation than the four countries of concern discussed above. Nonetheless, each has sought independent capabilities that would give it access to the nuclear material needed to make nuclear explosives, and each has avoided final international commitments not to make them.* Argentina has an unsafeguarded uranium enrichment facility (not yet in full operation) and is building a reprocessing plant that will not be safeguarded at all times. Brazil, in addition to safeguarded enrichment and reprocessing facilities being acquired from the Federal Republic of Germany, is reported to be building an unsafeguarded enrichment facility of a different type under military auspices. Thus, both appear intent on acquiring the *option* to develop nuclear explosives. But as yet, there is no convincing evidence that either has actually decided to exercise that option. Their motivation to do so seems weaker than that of any of the four countries discussed above, and the prospects for their participating in a regional nuclear-weapon-free zone (which has already been established by a treaty that both have at least signed) seem considerably brighter.

As between the two, Argentina has seemed the more likely to decide to develop nuclear weapons, but the Alfonsin administration ap-

---

* Other than their respective actions on the Treaty of Tlatelolco, described in the foot-note on p. 22.

pears quite unlikely to make such a decision. However, the other daunting political problems faced by that administration make it doubtful that Argentina will soon enter into firm international commitments against proliferation. In these circumstances, there are tactical questions as to how hard Argentina should be pressed to do so at this time, while recognizing that future Argentine governments might rekindle the proliferation risk.

In the absence of an Argentine decision to acquire nuclear explosives, a Brazilian decision to do so also seems unlikely in the near future, despite occasional disquieting statements by Brazilian military officials and speculation in the Brazilian press.

Non-proliferation objectives for these two countries should be:

(a) to foster an assessment by each that the acquisition of nuclear explosives (including any purporting to be for "peaceful" purposes) would not be in its net interest;

(b) to achieve Argentine ratification of the Limited Test Ban Treaty and of the Treaty of Tlatelolco as soon as politically feasible, and meanwhile to obtain an acceptable resolution of its dispute with the International Atomic Energy Agency over the terms of the safeguards agreement required by the latter treaty;

(c) to obtain the fullest possible safeguards coverage of Argentine and Brazilian nuclear activities (including comprehensive safeguards under the Treaty of Tlatelolco) and, possibly, arrangements for mutual inspection of all nuclear facilities in both countries;

(d) to secure an explicit dedication of the Argentine and Brazilian enrichment facilities to the production of low-enriched uranium;

(e) to head off a nuclear explosion by either country, even under the guise of one for "peaceful" purposes; and

(f) to persuade each country to exercise prudence in its nuclear exports and to adopt appropriate supply conditions so as to avoid its becoming a source of further proliferation. (In this connection the recent Argentine announcement that it would require IAEA safeguards on all its nuclear exports is encouraging.)

Further security commitments or assurances from third parties, even if obtainable, do not seem necessary in these two cases, since (1) neither country poses a military threat to the other or faces an external threat to which nuclear weapons seem relevant; and (2) both are already parties to the Rio Treaty, a mutual security pact to which the United States is also a party. Assurances from the nuclear weapon states that they will not use or threaten to use nuclear weapons against these Latin American countries could be obtained automatically by joining the Treaty of Tlatelolco, whose Protocol II on that subject has been ratified by all five nuclear weapon states.

Since the United States government provides no significant bilateral economic aid or military grants or credits to Argentina or Brazil, the prospect of losing such benefits (pursuant to the non-proliferation provisions of the Foreign Assistance Act) does not currently provide a disincentive to further proliferatory activities by these countries.

Two factors lessen the impact of approaches to these two countries based on international nuclear cooperation: (1) their reduced interest in major new nuclear transactions because of their financial difficulties; and (2) the fact that the United States is now barred by its own legislation from any significant nuclear cooperation with them. But both Argentina and Brazil have an interest in not jeopardizing the supplies and services that are still needed from other nuclear suppliers for the completion, operation, and maintenance of existing nuclear facilities. This partial continued dependence provides an opportunity for other suppliers (such as the Federal Republic of Germany and Canada) to ensure maximum safeguards coverage in these countries. Moreover, the completion of unsafeguarded, indigenous, sensitive nuclear facilities by Argentina or Brazil can at least be impeded and delayed by concerted action of foreign suppliers.

At first blush, the staggering international debt faced by the two countries would appear to provide a source of leverage, enabling the United States to point out that debt relief would be facilitated if they avoid further proliferatory actions and impaired if they proceed with such actions. But, in using this argument, one must recognize that an actual denial of debt relief to these countries would undermine their new civilian regimes, which are less likely to exercise the nuclear weapons option than their military predecessors; and that it could lead to default on their obligations, with dire consequences for the international monetary system and banking institutions in the creditor nations.

The insistence of both countries on retaining the option to develop nuclear explosives for "peaceful" purposes is a major stumbling block. It is holding up an Argentine full-scope safeguards agreement with the IAEA, which it insists upon settling before ratifying the Treaty of Tlatelolco. Exercise of the peaceful nuclear explosions option by either country would be seen as a serious latent military threat to the other. Yet neither country appears to have any actual program or plans for the development of explosives for this purpose. In these circumstances, further efforts should be made to convince them of the severe limitations of "peaceful" nuclear explosions and to seek a mutual moratorium on their development, or at least acknowledgement that neither has current plans to develop such explosives and each would consult the other and the IAEA before instituting such development.

Another potentially important approach would be through test ban treaties. Argentina should be urged to ratify the Limited Test Ban Treaty (which it has only signed). The Threshold Test Ban Treaty and related Treaty on Peaceful Nuclear Explosions are not helpful in this regard, since they are not even open for adherence by non-nuclear weapon states. But if a comprehensive test ban treaty could be agreed upon by the superpowers—unlikely as that appears at this time—the prospects seem good that Argentina and Brazil (which have consistently supported resolutions calling for such a treaty) would join it. (As noted above, Argentina's President recently joined in a plea for such a treaty.) If they did, it would help prevent their demonstration of a nuclear explosive capability, foreclose the development of more advanced nuclear explosives, and avert the risk of "peaceful" nuclear explosive programs by either country, and thus help provide the mutual reassurance needed to head off proliferation in this region.

Conclusion

The picture painted in this report may seem less alarmist than other assessments of near-term proliferation prospects (which focus primarily on capabilities and give little weight to offsetting legal and political factors). Yet this panel believes that complacency must be avoided as much as despair, since the probability of containing these proliferation risks is only slightly higher than of failing to do so; and that the potential perils of further proliferation are so great that its prevention must be a prime and constant security goal not only of the United States, but of the entire global community.

New Approaches to Non-Proliferation: A European Approach

Report of the NANPEA Steering Committee

Johan Jørgen Holst, Sergio Finzi, David Fischer,
Bertrand Goldschmidt, Simone Herpels,
Guenter Hildenbrand, Giorgio La Malfa, Peter Ludlow,
Sir Ronald Mason, Angel Viñas, and Harald Müller

Introduction

The present report constitutes the first comprehensive European statement on non-proliferation. In the past the European position has been expressed as reactions to or comments on US policy perspectives. This report is a consensus document; it is noteworthy that people with such varied backgrounds, experiences, responsibilities, and national identities were able to agree on a coherent and comprehensive policy statement about non-proliferation. The project was entitled "New Approaches to Non-Proliferation: A European Approach," suggesting a perceived need to explore new ground and novel departures.

In addition to the Steering Committee, the NANPEA project has comprised in-depth studies of the history and structure of non-proliferation policy in Western Europe, the policy perspectives and incentives of Argentina, Brazil, India, Iran, Israel, Pakistan, and South Africa, and the role of West European countries in influencing their calculations of interest, costs, and benefits. (These studies will all be published by CEPS). Special workshops were also arranged to examine the national perspectives in a regional context.

The deliberations of the European Steering Committee have been predicated on the belief that non-proliferation constitutes a foreign policy objective of the utmost importance — one which should unite rather than divide the international community. Western Europe and the democracies of North America have a shared interest in stopping nuclear proliferation. Further proliferation of nuclear weapons could threaten the stability of the prevailing international order and exacerbate the consequences of existing instabilities and rivalries.

In a certain sense one of the most remarkable outcomes of international relations over the last quarter of a century has been the relative absence of nuclear proliferation. When we compare the present situation with the dire predictions of the National Planning Association in the late 1950s, we find no confirmation of the pessimistic notions that matters would inevitably grow worse, or that what could go wrong would most certainly do so.

However, non-proliferation is not a law of nature; it is the result of deliberate policy and decisions. The results so far reflect in part the norms and policies which were developed in order to prevent proliferation. Furthermore, we must not resort to the fallacious conclusion that what has worked in the past will certainly work in the future, particularly in a future where many parameters of international relations are changing rapidly. Success is possible but far from inevitable.

We should approach the issues involved from the perspective that the environment within which non-proliferation policies will have to be implemented will be one of sovereign states. We shall have no international institution with the authority and means to enforce rules and norms of international behaviour. Nations will calculate their own interests, including their stakes in international order, and act on the basis of an assessment of costs and benefits, risks and options. Decisions concerning nuclear proliferation primarily will be decisions about national security, status, and prestige in a specific political context. Outside powers are able to affect the balance of incentives and disincentives, but they cannot dictate it.

Hence, the European approach to the international problem of nuclear proliferation has become one of co-option and cooperation rather than deprival and punishment, attempting to engage potential nuclear weapon states in the management of a non-proliferation regime. In such a regime the Non-Proliferation Treaty (NPT) is obviously a key element, but not the only one. Interaction rather than exclusion and the structuring of incentives rather than application of the penal code characterize the outlook of the European Steering Committee.

We should be aware of the pitfalls of self-righteousness, of course. West European nations were much slower to appreciate the dangers and systemic implications of nuclear proliferation than the Americans. Some of the controversies which arose across the Atlantic were the result of a lack of international perspective by European governments. However, times and attitudes are changing, and over the last fifteen years or so a rather coherent and consistent European policy profile has emerged. In our report we have attempted to outline its main features. We do not consider it a perfect policy, and we have some specific recommendations for how to improve it. But we believe that it is conceptually well founded and coherent, and that it is reasonably effective in an operational sense.

Non-proliferation is neither an all-or-nothing proposition nor a finite objective. It cannot be limited to stopping proliferation. If some proliferation should occur, careful attention must be paid to how the international community may be able to contain and limit the consequences, including stabilizing measures which could prevent or limit a further spread. Non-proliferation constitutes a policy objective which requires continuous and permanent management. It is a policy field where we must avoid letting the best become the enemy of the good.

The issue of nuclear proliferation has regional as well as global dimensions and implications. It must be dealt with at both levels, always recognizing that the two are interrelated. The issues are less tangible and the linkages less demonstrable at the global level. We know that there is a strong psychological linkage between vertical and horizontal proliferation. But we do not know very much about the specific connections and thresholds.

Nevertheless, it seems clear that the failure of the nuclear weapon states, and particularly the two superpowers, to contain and reverse their competition in nuclear arms affects the climate and atmosphere of relations between nuclear weapon states and non-nuclear weapon states. More importantly, it affects the legitimacy of the non-proliferation regime, particularly among third world countries. If the legitimacy of the regime is reduced, the political costs of a break-out will decrease, the threshold against proliferation may be lowered, and would-be proliferators may even be tempted to present a nuclear explosion as a victory for the principle of third world self-reliance. The non-proliferation regime will lose legitimacy to the extent that it is viewed as an imposed regime which involves constraints on the options of the "have-not" nations while the nuclear "haves" accept no constraints on their options. Hence the stalemate in East-West arms negotiations and the heavy focus on new weapon systems and novel dimensions of the arms competition tend to ease the political path for countries which want to enter the "big league" of the nuclear weapon states.

A stalemate in the efforts to develop more equitable North-South relations may also increase the symbolic significance of "entering the big league". The bitterness engendered by the outright hostility of some of the major industrial countries of the North to the quest for a new international economic order may have eased the political route to nuclear weapon status for countries within the Group of 77. Similarly, in a world of enormous inequities it will be increasingly difficult to retain acceptance of the implicit assumption that reliance on nuclear weapons by the rich countries of the North is compatible with the proposition that the countries of the South should forego the nuclear option. In a shrinking world double-standards will be subject to increased scrutiny.

Finally, with the introduction of very advanced conventional technologies, particularly for purposes of projecting power into distant areas, some third world countries could come to view nuclear weapons as a cost-effective means of preventing them from bridging the technological gap, particularly in the context of increased propensities in the policies of the "Great Powers" to intervene in the third world by military means. We therefore cannot escape the perspective that non-proliferation policies must be viewed in the context of the broad features and trends of international relations at large.

In regional terms, non-proliferation policies may be approached from the perspective of mutual confidence building. If we consider that the threshold countries will tend to view the nuclear option principally in security terms, reassurance becomes as important a theme as deterrence. The European Steering Committee considers the IAEA safeguards system a very important confidence-building mechanism. If competing nations recognize that regional nuclear monopoly is not a realistic objective, they may conclude that their interests are better served by reciprocal abstention. Safeguards contribute to their ability to exercise mutual restraint by providing credible evidence that would-be adversaries are not engaging in clandestine acquisition. In this context the European Steering Committee draws attention to the need to strengthen the IAEA, both financially and technologically.

A similar perspective may be applied to the consideration of regional nuclear-weapon-free zones. The Tlatelolco Treaty covering Latin America constitutes a pilot example, even if the construction is not yet complete. Such zones provide additional mechanisms for mutual reassurance and confidence building. However, a minimum amount of prior confidence must exist for nations to consider the establishment of nuclear-weapon-free zones.

It seems doubtful that the conditions can be met in the two areas most often discussed in this connection, Africa and the Middle East, due to the hostile relations between South Africa and the black Africans in the one instance and Israel and her Muslim neighbours in the other. Nuclear-weapon-free zones may be viewed by some states in the region concerned as means for particular countries to obtain international recognition rather than cope with the problem of nuclear proliferation. They may also be viewed as a means of freezing a comparative advantage for states like Israel and South Africa, which are often believed to have "bombs in the basement". Nuclear-weapon-free zones are probably incompatible with the maintenance of present postures of nuclear ambiguity and would require mechanisms for mutual inspection and reassurance.

It should be noted that nuclear-weapon-free zones in Europe are hardly relevant to the problem of nuclear proliferation due to the existence of three nuclear weapon states and the presence of US nuclear forces in the region. Schemes for nuclear-weapon-free zones there should be considered primarily from the perspective of regional political order and stability during crises.

Nuclear-weapon-free zones de-legitimize nuclear weapon programmes and deflate the perceived status and prestige pay-offs of going nuclear. However, we should recognize the interconnection between the legitimacy of the non-proliferation regime at the global level and at the level of regional politics. The normative content of nuclear-weapon-free zones could be seriously weakened if the global regime were to lose legitimacy due to conflicts in North-South relations in general and conflicts between nuclear weapon states and non-nuclear weapon states in particular.

The geographical delineation of regional nuclear-weapon-free zones will pose problems in some instances as the states of a given region may be concerned not only about regional rivalries but also about possible threats from extra-regional sources. South Asia is a case in point, as the security concerns and status considerations of India are not focused only on Pakistan but include the People's Republic of China. Similarly, Israel could be concerned about the impact of a Pakistani "Islamic bomb" on the political texture of the Middle East. In some instances confidence may be enhanced by bilateral or multilateral schemes for mutual surveillance of nuclear installations, perhaps aided as well by supplier states as interlocutors.

"Crazy-states" constitute a particular problem which must be dealt with on an *ad hoc* basis; prior international planning and consultation run the danger of being perceived as Northern state collusion and attempts to justify intervention and neo-colonialist ambitions. The issue of nuclear terrorism may not be as urgent as frequently thought; chemical and biological weapons appear to contain more of a clear and present danger in this context. However, the European Steering Committee strongly recommends that the EC countries ratify the convention on physical security of nuclear materials, thus causing the convention to enter into force.

Nuclear trade influences the availability of nuclear weapon options and contributes to the fear or confidence among neighbouring and competing states. The London Guidelines constitute an important element in the emerging non-proliferation regime and they are adhered to by all the important exporters in Europe, including the Federal Republic of Germany and France, which are the most important ones. The West European nations in general have not agreed to require full-scope safeguards as a condition for nuclear exports, primarily because some important recipient countries are not prepared to accept them. It is arguable that insistence on full-scope safeguards would stimulate trends toward autarky and remove important nations from the international regime of non-proliferation. Similarly, West European countries have refused to agree to an outright ban on the export of sensitive materials. However, they have accepted the formula of restraint, and in their export policies follow the practice of a pragmatic case-by-case consideration.

The long-term objective should be full-scope safeguards. The operational issue is how to get there in a way which is consistent with the constitution and management of a broadly accepted and respected non-proliferation regime. Of particular importance in this connection is the integration and cooperation of third-tier supplier states in the non-proliferation regime, bearing in mind that they include some of the "problem countries" from the point of view of nuclear proliferation.

A basic feature of a new approach to non-proliferation must be recognition that a viable non-proliferation regime will comprise a composite and complex set of norms, rules, and obligations. In addition to the NPT, such a regime will encompass *de facto* and *de jure* full-scope safeguards, partial safeguards, IAEA membership, regional nuclear-weapon-free zones, bilateral cooperation, regional cooperation (including multinational facilities), commercial and scientific relations, policies on nuclear arms negotiations, policies of mutual restraint in the use of force, policies designed to enhance more equitable economic relations in international society, etc.

The European nations have come a long way in shaping a coherent and concerted approach to non-proliferation, an approach which is heavily influenced by US thinking and policies. But it also exhibits some unique features which make it complementary to the American approach and contribute to flexibility in the international management of the emerging non-proliferation regime. To demonstrate the evolution of West European non-proliferation policy to the world, the Steering Committee recommends that a joint statement be made by the heads of state and government of the EC member countries which stresses common interest in nuclear non-proliferation.

The fact that we have seen little proliferation during the last decades may lead to dangerous complacency, to the conclusion that non-proliferation need not occupy a prominent spot on the diplomatic agenda. Such conclusions would be dangerous because they underestimate the volatility of international relations and the basic uncertainties concerning their future course and combustion. Too much attention may be focused on the "problem countries" of today at the expense of the possible challenges of future constellations.

In addition to focusing on specific countries and regions, the new approaches to non-proliferation must embrace strategies for general deterrence, reassurance, and reward — attempting to take the potential "profit" out of proliferation. Sanctions should be approached cautiously in view of the rather bleak record of international sanctions and the debilitating consequences of trying to spell out commitments beforehand. Furthermore, nations should eschew sanctions which tend to legitimize the use of nuclear weapons as instruments of war or political coercion. Non-proliferation depends on less reliance on nuclear weapons for the conduct of international relations and for national security.

Oslo, April 1985   Johan Jørgen Holst

I. Non-proliferation: the political perspective

1. Nuclear proliferation remains one of the gravest threats to world peace. Vertical proliferation contributes to the development of increasingly sophisticated weapons, which always pose the danger of being used; horizontal proliferation (additional countries acquiring nuclear weapons) bears the risk that some conventional conflicts may end in nuclear exchanges. While the main thrust of our study is directed at horizontal proliferation, vertical proliferation and its consequences are taken into account.

   Horizontal proliferation, as we understand it, consists of many steps towards a full-fledged, operational nuclear force. The first explosion is the most *visible* step in the process; but the decision to progress through a series of tests is the most *significant* step. Non-proliferation policy should be directed at preventing or dissuading countries from taking these steps.

2. As frequently stated by their governments, West European countries share the interest of the international community that the spread of nuclear weapons be stopped. This common European interest should make non-proliferation a preferred field of unified action. As the member states of the European Communities strive to develop a joint approach in selected fields of foreign and security policy, non-proliferation could be one which fosters both unity among EC members and cooperation between them and their non-EC West European neighbours.

3. A unified West European voice would considerably strengthen the attempts of the world community to work for the common good of non-proliferation. In particular, the growing danger of polarization of the non-proliferation debate between the super-powers and the "have nots" could be lowered by a unified West European approach.

   While belonging to the North, Western Europe bears no image of being a superpower and has no record of a strict policy of denial in nuclear trade. Moreover, it has special historical and economic links with many of the countries causing concern. Western Europe therefore has the opportunity to contribute to the evolution of the global non-proliferation consensus. This contribution should be based on the following general considerations.

4. *Non-proliferation policy must create a strong international regime* which can evolve and adapt to changes in nuclear developments as well as in world politics.* Since the beginning of non-proliferation efforts, the regime has had to cope with the inevitable world-wide growth of technical capabilities and with the appearance of new regional powers. Any attempts to "freeze" the regime at a particular point must fail; the management of a continuously changing nuclear scene will remain a permanent task. One challenge will be to integrate into the international regime the third world states which emerge as future suppliers of nuclear technology, equipment, and materials.

5. The proliferation of nuclear weapons is basically the result of governments' assessments of the balance of incentives and disincentives for developing them, with perceptions of national security playing the dominant role. *Non-proliferation policy should aim to influence this balance at the margin.* A non-proliferation regime contributes to this objective by providing reassurances that other countries will not take the road to nuclear weapons acquisition. In this sense it should not be viewed as a "police" regime, but as a system of mutual confidence-building based on international safeguards.

6. *The non-proliferation regime must be compatible with the principle of sovereignty and equality of states.* It will not be sustainable in the long run if policies are forced upon participants; it must be based on their voluntary accession.

The Non-Proliferation Treaty (NPT) constitutes just such a voluntary sovereign commitment by its non-nuclear parties to renounce the nuclear option. (See Appendix B.) It also comprises a commitment by the nuclear weapon states to reduce their nuclear arsenals.

The emerging international regime involves bargains between nuclear and non-nuclear weapon states, between suppliers and recipients of nuclear materials and technologies. The fair balance of obligations and benefits emerging from those bargains is a key ingredient in the regime's ability to survive. The discriminatory aspects implied by the different statuses of the participants in those bargains will not be eliminated overnight. But as far as

---

* *By regime* we refer to a pattern of institutions, rules, norms, and guidelines — informal as well as formal — which guide policy in an issue area such as nuclear non-proliferation. It is not necessarily universal. A *regime* in this sense is thus more comprehensive and less binding than a legal or constitutional system. For further elaboration of our view of the present non-proliferation regime, see § 34 and § 35.

possible the regime must credibly project the prospect that these aspects might be reduced over time and will certainly not increase.

7. While proliferation is mainly an issue of national security, nuclear trade influences the availability of options and contributes to fear or confidence among neighbours. These effects of nuclear commerce become more marginal as a country's nuclear programme approaches the stage of self-sufficiency. Thus *safeguards and guidelines for nuclear trade function as confidence-building instruments and are indispensable building blocks of a non-proliferation regime.*

Ideally the safeguards and guidelines should apply to all states equally. However, such equality is rendered impossible by the present position of nuclear weapon states and the refusal of some states to accept full-scope safeguards as being in their national interest; compromise solutions must be sought.

8. The trend to apply safeguards to increasing numbers of civilian facilities in more nuclear weapon states points in the right direction, as it diminishes the discrimination of differing safeguard burdens.

As for export policies, *supplier countries should do their best to convince recipients that full-scope safeguards are in their own best interests.* If such attempts fail, suppliers should try to come as close to an ideal safeguards solution as possible.

9. Nuclear proliferation is embedded in broader issues of international politics. *East-West tensions and any concomitant acceleration of the arms race are detrimental to the maintenance of the non-proliferation regime.* They enhance the general feeling of insecurity among nations and in some cases contribute directly to the security concerns of individual countries. The growth and mounting sophistication of nuclear arsenals intensify the frustrations resulting from the basic discrimination between nuclear and non-nuclear weapon states and forcefully project the image of the utility of nuclear weapons.

10. *Non-proliferation is also inevitably placed in the political arena of North-South relations.* If dissatisfaction about the course of the economic and political dialogue between developing and industrialized countries grows, third world states may increasingly view the renunciation of sovereign rights, as implied by the non-proliferation regime and particularly the NPT, as a restrictive unilateral political liability. The non-proliferation regime would

then be threatened by erosion of consensus on still another front.

It is important to keep this interrelationship between broader world order issues and non-proliferation in mind; compartmentalized decision-making in foreign policy often makes it difficult for officials to be aware of such connections between apparently different and separate political issues. This is another reason why non-proliferation should be more prominent on the political agenda in Western Europe.

II. Nuclear policy in Western Europe: convergence and divergence

11. Any European approach to non-proliferation must take into account the convergence and divergence within the region in the nuclear field.

    Western Europe includes countries which have shown the greatest faith in civilian uses of nuclear energy, particularly in recent years. France already produces about 60% of its electricity from uranium and Belgium 50%. Finland, Sweden, and Switzerland have reached or passed the 40% mark, while the Federal Republic of Germany (FRG) now produces 28% of its electricity in this way.

    On the other hand, Denmark, Greece, Iceland, Luxembourg, and Norway have no nuclear power programmes at present. Turkey is considering the purchase of her first station, while a 1978 referendum has prevented Austria from starting-up its single completed unit. Sweden has decided to limit its plans to 12 units, with operations phased out by 2010.

    Four European countries (France, Portugal, Spain, and Sweden) have notable domestic uranium resources. In addition French, FRG, and UK companies own or hold shares in substantial resources in Africa, Australia, and Canada.

12. All of the EC member states are *ipso facto* members of the European Community of Atomic Energy (Euratom), which resulted from the 1957 Rome Treaty. The Commission of the EC, which administers the Euratom Treaty, ensures the services of the nuclear materials supply agency, implements a nuclear free market in the Community, ensures appropriate international relationships with third countries and international organizations, and assumes responsibility for the Euratom safeguards system, which is coordinated with IAEA inspections following a 1973 agreement between Euratom and the IAEA.

    The Commission has also developed a nuclear research programme, which is partly executed in its Joint Research Centre.

13. In the 1960s, thirteen European countries acquired the technology of reprocessing spent fuel and separating plutonium through their participation in Eurochemic, a joint undertaking located in Belgium and created under the aegis of the OECD. (The UK was already advanced in the field.)

France presently owns the only commercial reprocessing facility in the world for light water reactor fuel and has contracts with several European countries (the FRG, Switzerland, and Sweden). The UK is building a similar facility and the FRG will start construction in 1985, while Belgium has decided to reactivate the Eurochemic plant. (The project was closed in the mid-1970s for financial reasons.) On the back-end of the fuel cycle, the majority of the interested European countries lean towards the reprocessing solution with recycling of plutonium in power reactors, while Sweden is in favour of indefinite storage of the spent fuel.

In 1980 the Council of Ministers of the European Community approved three resolutions in favour of developing reprocessing technology and fast breeder reactors, as well as launching a Community policy in the field of nuclear waste management. Belgium, France, the FRG, Italy, and the UK have decided to pool their efforts in developing the fast breeder reactor system for commercial purposes.

14. In the late 1970s Western Europe moved towards independence in the field of uranium enrichment through two multinational enrichment enterprises: Urenco (FRG, Netherlands, UK) and Eurodif (Belgium, France, Italy, Spain). The only West European nations that have nuclear power plants but are not included in these enterprises are Finland, Sweden, and Switzerland. Because of present excess capacity of the two joint enterprises, Europe now competes with the US and USSR on the world market for sales of enriched uranium.

15. The US nuclear industry was helped initially by its technical advance in the light-water reactor field, the monopoly of enriched uranium sales, and by the US-Euratom agreement in the early 1960s. It therefore gained a major part of the European market in nuclear power plants at that time. Today Belgium, France, the FRG, Italy, and the UK are able to offer their services in the various steps of the nuclear fuel cycle to the world market. But to date the only exporters of nuclear power plants have been the UK (with its first two sales in 1958 but none since), Sweden (with a single export to Finland), and the FRG and France (which are now the US's most successful competitors on the world market).

16. Only two European countries, the UK and France, have military nuclear programmes. The UK exploded nuclear weapons for the first time in 1952 and France in 1960. In terms of warheads, their

arsenals are now only a small fraction of the US or Soviet ones, but are being substantially modernized and expanded.

17. France and the UK are also the only West European countries building nuclear submarines for their navies. The FRG built a nuclear merchant ship for civilian use in the 1960s, but this went out of service in 1979.

18. France is the only West European country not party to the Partial Nuclear Test Ban Treaty of 1963. However, since 1974 its weapons tests have taken place underground in the Pacific atolls.

   France and Spain are not parties to the Non-Proliferation Treaty of Nuclear Weapons (NPT). In 1968 France announced that it would act like a party to the treaty and has since voluntarily agreed to put some of its peaceful activities under IAEA safeguards. Spain has done the same for any facility which was not already submitted to such control.

   The UK has voluntarily submitted all of her peaceful activities to IAEA safeguards.

19. Austria, the FRG, Finland, and Italy were obliged to renounce the military option as a consequence of the treaties following World War II. This condition was included in the 1947 peace treaties with Finland and Italy and the 1955 treaty with Austria.

   Until the FRG's signature of the NPT in 1969, its renunciation was in the form of a letter from Chancellor Adenauer annexed to the 1954 Treaty of the Western European Union, which includes the initial six EC members and the UK. This treaty provides for a control of the signatories' stocks of nuclear weapons deployed on the continent, but such control has never been applied. In 1954 the FRG also joined the North Atlantic Treaty Organization (NATO).

20. The NATO alliance, the presence of US nuclear weapons in many non-nuclear weapon West European countries, the British and French nuclear deterrent forces, and the compulsory renunciation by Italy, the FRG, Austria, and Finland are all factors specific to the region which have encouraged its other non-nuclear weapons states to rally round the NPT. Thus they have abandoned the military option and have agreed to place all of their nuclear activities under IAEA safeguards. This unique combination of factors favouring adherence to the non-proliferation regime does not exist in other regions.

III. The evolution of consensus in Western Europe

21. Whatever their differences, all the West European countries have a joint interest in both the decrease of vertical proliferation and the inhibition of horizontal proliferation. This interest stems from their commitment to international order and the growing convergence of their foreign policies, reflecting *inter alia* their geopolitical situation between the two superpowers, their special relationship with the less privileged countries of the world, and their increasing role in international nuclear relations. Furthermore, non-proliferation is a major political objective in each of the countries. Any common European policy on an important political objective is a step towards European unification as well as an asset in pursuing the objective.

22. By their adherence to the NPT — or in the case of France, through appropriate policy — the European countries took a first major step towards a common non-proliferation approach. In particular, Articles III and IV of the NPT had direct implications for their future conduct of international nuclear relations.

    Article III obliges them not to provide source or special fissionable material or equipment, or material especially designed or prepared for the processing, use, or production of special fissionable material, to any non-nuclear weapon state for peaceful purposes "unless the source or special fissionable material is subject to IAEA safeguards". All of the nuclear supplier signatories of the treaty jointly prepared a list of material and equipment which should automatically trigger IAEA safeguards when exported to a non-nuclear weapon state (the so-called Zangger list).

    Article IV spells out the unalienable right of signatories to develop research, production, and use of atomic energy for peaceful purposes; it also commits them to participate in the fullest possible exchange of equipment, materials, and scientific and technological information for the peaceful use of nuclear energy.

    The preamble and Article VI also oblige the nuclear-weapon signatories to continue negotiations for "general and complete disarmament", and movement towards the total prohibition of nuclear weapon tests.

23. The 1973 oil crisis, the 1974 Indian nuclear explosion, the announcement that several third world countries (including

Middle Eastern ones) intended to embark on ambitious nuclear programmes, and the fact that West European countries (particularly the FRG and France) were now competing with the US for a share of the world market in nuclear power plants led to restructured approaches to non-proliferation.

Until the early 1970s, US dominance of nuclear world markets coincided with US leadership in non-proliferation policy. As West European states emerged as major suppliers, they were obliged to pay more attention to non-proliferation as a foreign policy objective.

24. The new approach was negotiated in London between 1975 and 1978 among a group of the main nuclear suppliers. The West European countries joining the final agreement were Belgium, France, the FRG, Italy, the Netherlands, Sweden, Switzerland, and the UK. (See Appendix D.)

One result of these negotiations was that France for the first time formally relinquished the advantages previously derived from freedom of choice over political conditions to be attached to her nuclear sales. Like all the other members of the group, France accepted application of IAEA safeguards to all future exports of items on an agreed list of materials, equipment, and technological information. This list was slightly more extensive than the Zangger list.

25. During these negotiations a majority of West European suppliers developed a common position towards the more far-reaching demands of the US, Canada, and Australia. Most West European countries, while persuaded by the plea that new initiatives were needed, declined to accept full-scope safeguards as a precondition of their nuclear exports. They also refused to agree to an outright ban on the export of sensitive materials. But they accepted the formula of "restraint" on those exports. Eventually, in 1977, France and the FRG agreed to stop exports of reprocessing plants and technologies "for the time-being". Existing contracts — meaning the one between the FRG and Brazil — were to be excluded from this restriction.

26. The evolution of a West European consensus continued through the International Nuclear Fuel Cycle Evaluation (INFCE). While not unanimous in their degree of assertiveness and their inclination to compromise, West European governments defended their interest in closing the fuel-cycle option and opening the breeder reactor one as no more proliferation-prone than the once-through cycle or various fuel cycle alternatives.

They insisted that a more cooperative attitude towards recipient countries would eventually prove a better tool for fostering non-proliferation than a policy of denial which would go beyond the London Guidelines.

27. At the same time, EC member states worked together in their reaction to the US Nuclear Non-Proliferation Act (NNPA) of 1978. Among other things this law called for the right of the US government to give case-by-case prior consent to the reprocessing of fuel of US origin and stipulated the renegotiation of all existing fuel supply contracts. This also concerned the Euratom-US agreement. Euratom member countries have so far agreed to refuse the NNPA's *prior consent* request and the requirement to renegotiate the old agreement. Eventually their attitude led to an annual presidential waiver on the termination of the agreement, as required by the NNPA.

28. Recently West European nuclear exporters, in particular France and the FRG, developed regular mutual consultations on nuclear export policy. At Community level the need for coordination of non-proliferation policy has also been accepted. In December 1981, an EC Working Group on Non-Proliferation was established, and it has met regularly since then.

The group is designed to harmonize policies under the umbrella of European Political Cooperation (EPC), the regular consultations of the foreign affairs ministers of EC countries. To date the most important achievement of this Working Group has been the agreement to apply the London Guidelines Community-wide. (See Appendix E.) This agreement brings the nuclear export policies of EC nuclear suppliers in closer harmony with the 1957 Rome Treaties and closes a loop-hole in nuclear export policy.

29. Over the past fifteen years, non-proliferation policy in Western Europe has converged to a certain extent, but it remains the prerogative of national governments. However, the evolution of consensus shows there is a basis for intensified and expanded coordination. For example, the London Guidelines have provided a sound base for a joint approach, despite their initial unpopularity among some recipient countries.

30. Because memberships of the West European regional organizations vary and do not always overlap, collaboration will obviously be multi-layered.

Continued consultation among EC nuclear supplier countries, particularly France and the Federal Republic of Germany (the major exporters of power reactors today), will remain the core of West European cooperation. Reports by the Working Group on Non-Proliferation should make this issue a routine subject on the agenda of European Political Cooperation, even in the absence of dramatic proliferation events. In the same way, non-proliferation policy should be a regular issue on the agenda when the European heads of government meet to prepare for the western Summit meetings.

31. It is essential that coordination extend beyond the boundaries of the EC. While the recent OECD agreement on nuclear export financing does not directly relate to non-proliferation, it provides additional rules for nuclear exports, facilitates coordination of export policies, and includes all West European countries as well as the other industrialized states.

Outside the EC, Finland, Switzerland, and Sweden are already applying the London Guidelines. Spain and Portugal should accede to the Guidelines when they enter the EC and participate in the Working Group on Non-Proliferation. It would be useful if the remaining West European countries (Austria and Norway) could be included in some consultative framework.

32. WEU member countries have recently expressed interest in enhanced efforts to coordinate arms control policy. Non-proliferation is a subject which should be high on the agenda of the WEU's Agency for the Control of Armaments. Analysis of the arms control implications of non-proliferation policy within WEU would be a valuable supplement to the export-policy work of the EPC Working Group.

The NATO Arms Control Experts Committee constitutes the appropriate place for coordination with the other West European members of the alliance, the US, and Canada.

IV. Steps to strengthen the non-proliferation regime

33. Non-proliferation policy consists of two separate yet interrelated tasks:

    • strengthening the consensus on the general policy principles, norms, and institutions which comprise the non-proliferation regime, and

    • dealing carefully, on a case-by-case basis, with the "problem countries" which are most inclined to develop nuclear weapons and are least integrated into the present regime.

    To the extent that the regime is strengthened, the threshold for a decision to breach the non-proliferation norm will become considerably higher. But it will never become insurmountable if the highest national interests of a country are seen to be at stake.

34. Efforts to strengthen the non-proliferation regime must avoid two fallacies. The first is identifying the non-proliferation regime entirely with the Non-Proliferation Treaty and thus dividing the world into two groups: NPT parties and non-parties. This definition would be overly simplistic.

    The non-proliferation regime is broader than the NPT. It covers *de facto* and *de jure* full-scope safeguards, partial (object-related) safeguards, IAEA membership, regional treaties (like the Tlatelolco Treaty*, establishing a nuclear-weapon-free zone in Latin America), bilateral cooperation (like the Argentina-Brazil agreement), and commercial and scientific relationships. Hence the non-proliferation regime can be conceived as a network which is tightest at the centre — the NPT — and becomes looser as it extends to its outer parts. The basic connections are still there. While continued and increased subscription to the NPT remains an important task, there is also a variety of other measures which could strengthen the regime.

35. The second fallacy is the extreme call for a regime which is technically and legally foolproof and the concomitant criticism that the NPT is not universal, that it allows for retreat from the

---

* Today all but five Latin American countries have signed and ratified this treaty and also waived the requirement that all other Latin American states have to do so for the treaty to come into force. Cuba and Guyana have not signed; Argentina has signed but not ratified; Brazil and Chile have signed and ratified but not accepted the waiver.

Treaty, that safeguards do not prevent diversion, etc. All these allegations are based on the mistaken belief that we can have a nuclear "police" regime in the absence of world government.

As long as international relations are founded on nation-states as the basic actors, no regime in any field of policy is fully secure. Regimes must be understood as erecting barriers which influence the interests of states at the margin. That states may act against the regime's norms in situations of superior national interest cannot be prevented. The plea for a perfect non-proliferation regime — and refusal to accept anything less — is the "best" acting as the enemy of the "good". Instead, incremental steps to strengthen the existing regime are necessary and sensible.

36. A joint statement on non-proliferation by the heads of state of the EC member states would be such a step. It could

  - emphasize European support for the objective of non-proliferation,

  - express satisfaction that no additional countries have acquired nuclear weapons for twenty years,

  - affirm the hope that this "state of affairs" can be maintained,

  - stress that nuclear testing by any of the present non-nuclear weapon states would be viewed with deep concern by the EC governments,

  - confirm their readiness to increased cooperation in the peaceful use of nuclear energy, particularly in the developing world.

If issued before the 1985 NPT Review Conference, such a statement would improve the climate for non-proliferation policy in the near future. Simultaneously, it would signal to potential proliferators that the Community countries are genuinely committed to non-proliferation. This would act as an additional barrier to crossing the threshold.

37. The IAEA remains an indispensable and authoritative instrument for implementing non-proliferation policy and should continue to receive the full backing of West European governments. In particular, the safeguarding function of the IAEA must be supported and the introduction of state-of-the-art technology be facilitated.

38. Research and development activities are essential in order to improve the effectiveness and efficiency of safeguards. Euratom's research activities on safeguard methodologies and instruments, complemented by the efforts of the individual countries, are also very helpful in this respect and should be continued and enlarged.

39. A balance must be maintained between the IAEA's safeguarding activities and its other main task, technical assistance. A steady increase in the resources available for such assistance will help to make the non-proliferation regime more acceptable to third world countries, particularly at a time when many of their own programmes are in financial difficulties. Ways should also be explored of specifically earmarking more technical assistance resources to countries that have accepted the regime.

40. Favourable treatment should be given to the concept of multinational facilities. The exploratory work of the IAEA on such facilities proved rather disappointing. Reasons for this disappointment were the difficulties inherent in the management of such enterprises, the changed market conditions which clearly worked against them, and a lack of interest by developing countries. However, this kind of international cooperation offers hope for sound confidence-building and deserves support.

European experiences reveal that multinational fuel cycle facilities can work satisfactorily if they are based on the mutual economic interests of the participants. There are few prospects for large multinational fuel-cycle facilities under international control in the foreseeable future. But the revival of similar ventures at the regional level, as an autonomous activity of the states involved (e.g. in Latin America), should not be excluded. Europe should be prepared to encourage and to support such developments.

41. A step forward would be the ratification of the convention on physical security of nuclear materials by Euratom and its member states. This would bring the number of ratifying countries above the 21 needed for the convention to enter into force. Ratification in the first half of 1985 would therefore improve the regime and give a positive signal to the NPT Review Conference. The convention could also serve as a means of reducing the threat of nuclear terrorism.

42. Including emerging suppliers in the non-proliferation regime is a major important task of the future. While the hardware, technology, and services they can offer at present are still small,

their capabilities will grow. Moveover, even small-size items can pose proliferation problems.

In 1984, South Africa's announcement that it would apply the London Guidelines to its nuclear exports and China's announced intention to ask for IAEA safeguards on exported items were heartening news. In general, there is no convincing evidence that new suppliers have assisted other countries in acquiring a nuclear weapons capability. Indeed, those countries have no distinct interest in the anarchic spread of nuclear capabilities. However, whether they approach the problem with benign neglect or with conscious responsibility makes a great deal of difference.

The latter attitude would certainly be fostered by an atmosphere of cooperation rather than confrontation. New suppliers should be drawn into a network of suppliers' consultations. Because of their cooperative record in nuclear export policy, European countries could well use their bilateral nuclear and diplomatic ties to initiate and sustain such a dialogue.

43. The NPT comes up for extension in 1995. As an indispensible ingredient of the regime, all efforts should be made to sustain the treaty beyond this date.

Given the present differences and dissatisfaction among the NPT parties, this will not be an easy task. Ten years is a very long period for diplomats dealing with day-to-day problems, so it is essential that a focused, long-term effort be made to concentrate some foreign policy resources on sustaining the NPT. This applies to *all* West European countries — even those which are not parties to the treaty but subscribe to its goals.

V. Export policy

44. In the 1970s it sometimes seemed that nuclear export policy was the single most important field for non-proliferation policy. Certainly this heavy emphasis overburdened the issue, as it underrated the importance of security aspects and the impact of broader international problems. However, if put in the right perspective, nuclear export policy remains a significant part of any non-proliferation policy: it can contribute to or detract from confidence-building, and add to or reduce satisfaction with the regime.

45. In dealing with export policy, one has to acknowledge the present market situation. The optimistic early- to mid-1970s forecasts on the growth of nuclear power have not materialized. However the reduced size of nuclear programmes has neither led to the disappearance of non-proliferation problems nor to unrestrained competition among suppliers for shrinking markets, with no regard to proliferation consequences.

   There is a continuing depression in international nuclear markets. Few reactor units will be ordered by countries of "proliferation concern" in the near future. There is no demand for additional enrichment capacity and, outside of Japan, no demand for commercially-sized reprocessing plants. This allows the non-proliferation regime some breathing space, but it does not eliminate the need to prepare for the "litmus test" of export policy when demand grows again at some time in the future.

46. Full-scope safeguards remain the long-term goal for non-proliferation-oriented export policy. The non-proliferation regime would be stronger if all civilian nuclear activities were under international safeguards. In negotiating export contracts, one should try to come as close to this goal as possible.

   However, it should be recognized that at present some recipient countries are not prepared to accept full-scope safeguards. When devising export policy one must be fully aware of the serious dilemma that might arise when applying general rules to this situation.

47. Outright denial of nuclear exports to non-full-scope safeguard importers would have the advantages of:
    - putting a clear choice before them,
    - creating a clear and visible advantage for being in or acceding to a full-scope safeguards position, and

- diminishing the risks of abuse of nuclear exports.

On the other hand, denial policies

- would not prevent the more advanced recipient countries from acquiring the materials and/or technologies needed to manufacture nuclear explosives — they already possess these capabilities;
- might exacerbate trends away from the international nuclear regime and towards autarky;
- could increase dissatisfaction with the non-proliferation regime, particularly the inequalities which it embodies, resulting in nuclear export policies which become part of a policy of defiance.

48. Not insisting on full-scope safeguards but requiring safeguards on exported items and their products would have the advantages of

- reaping the possible fruits of cooperation by establishing working relations,
- fostering a climate in which the recipient might be drawn closer to the non-proliferation regime,
- bringing at least part of the recipients' nuclear activities under safeguards, and
- reducing the motivation for autarky.

On the other hand, such policies would

- abolish tangible incentives to accept or to continue accepting full-scope safeguards,
- increase the possibility that nuclear exports would be abused.

49. There is no easy way out of this dilemma. It calls for flexibility and a thorough study of the case in question. It is unlikely that a general rule beyond the London Guidelines would be possible. The Guidelines are a great achievement because they establish clear and uniform rules which greatly reduce the danger of the kind of competition that would foster proliferation. While the implementation can and will be improved by refined lists of items triggering safeguards, the Guidelines need no amendment in the sense of a general rule.

What is needed is the development of a pragmatic code of conduct* for applying the Guidelines on a case-by-case basis, particularly where they concern safeguard requirements and restraint on the export of sensitive facilities. This code of conduct has to deal with the scope of export conditions, the types of items to be exported, and the recipient country.

50. The conditions attached to nuclear exports will vary from case to case. Short of full-scope safeguards, item safeguards with a replication clause for sensitive facilities (effecting safeguards for any facility of the same type constructed by the recipient) will be in order. In some cases the question of economic justification may have to be discussed. The appropriate criteria are the sensitivity of the item supplied and the record of the respective recipient. Applying such judgment is in no way an abuse of technological superiority. It is the suppliers' responsibility within a non-proliferation regime to do their very best to prevent the misuse of exports.

51. It must be recognized that proliferation sensitivity varies with the product supplied. Products are more sensitive if they require or yield large quantities of weapons-grade material, i.e. highly enriched uranium or plutonium with a fissile content of more than 90%.

Research facilities involving very small quantities of fissionable materials are at the lowest level of sensitivity. Light-water power reactors follow. They yield plutonium which, while theoretically usable for an explosive device after reprocessing, is of low quality for reliable, operational nuclear weapons and demands sophisticated technology for conversion for military use. To receive higher-quality plutonium, the fuel must be burned for shorter periods than economically justifiable. This exercise involves high costs and is highly visible, as it requires light-water reactors to be shut-down after brief periods of operation.

52. Natural uranium reactors, the heavy water required as moderator, and facilities for producing heavy water are somewhat more sensitive. They permit the brief burn-up and continuous withdrawal of fuel while the reactor is in operation. This activity involves lower cost penalties and is not highly visible, thereby creating some opportunity for covert action. However with adequate efforts and the latest technology, safeguarding is possible.

---

* By *code of conduct* we do not mean written, formal rules, but rather a tacit understanding of common behaviour which evolves from intensive consultations and growing experience in applying the London Guidelines.

At the high end of sensitivity are the supply of reprocessing and enrichment facilities and their technology and the supply of weapons-grade fissile material for larger size research reactors.

53. The usual rule would be that as the sensitivity of the items grows, export conditions would become more demanding. For power reactors, particularly the LWR, and small research units, object-related safeguards would not be entirely satisfactory from a non-proliferation point of view; but in some cases they may be the best that can be obtained at this time and an acceptable compromise.

There could be a presumption of full-scope safeguards as well as proven economic justification in particular cases. It is possible that in some cases no export would take place at all — depending to some degree on the recipient and its international credibility.

54. Particularly for more sensitive items, the bias of approving exports would be in favour of countries accepting full-scope safeguards. For other countries, the capability of constructing the respective unit in the near future by themselves would be a factor to be considered.

Moreover, sensitive exports should be treated with great restraint

- *if the recipient country is located in a war zone (or one of dangerous international tension).* In such cases, nuclear exports could arouse sensitivities and may even attract pre-emptive strikes, as demonstrated in Iraq in 1981. Exporting countries bear an obligation to see to it that their commercial interest does not exacerbate violent conflicts.

- *if the commitment of the recipient country to international law is in doubt, notwithstanding its non-proliferation undertakings.* This applies if the country has breached legal obligations in the past, if it is a supporter of terrorism, or if its leadership has issued ambiguous statements on the purposes of its nuclear programme.

55. Within the framework of the London Guidelines, nuclear exports will be conducted prudently on a case-by-case basis. The considerations proposed above should be relevant if particular

cases are under review. It is recognized that broader foreign policy goals will be taken into account in addition to purely nuclear non-proliferation aspects. In any case, continued close consultation on major export activities is required among West European suppliers.

VI. Arms control and disarmament

56. A persistent and increasing threat to a viable non-proliferation regime has been the ongoing arms race, particularly between the two superpowers. The failure to halt the build-up of ever more sophisticated nuclear weapons, or at least to convey to the rest of the world a realistic hope that this could be achieved in the near future, is increasingly seen by many non-nuclear weapon states as an act of bad faith which undermines the basic bargain of non-proliferation.

   This development is likely to come to the forefront of non-proliferation policy as the termination date of the NPT approaches. If this trend continues, the decline of the NPT — and moreover the breakdown of the whole non-proliferation regime — cannot be excluded as a possibility. It is therefore essential that the nuclear weapon states soon give unambiguous and credible proof that a serious change in policy is to be expected (preferably before the next NPT Review Conference in autumn 1985).

57. The conclusion of a Comprehensive Test Ban Treaty (CTBT) would be a highly visible step towards this objective. Putting an end to all nuclear weapon testing would significantly slow down — although not entirely foreclose — the innovative process of nuclear weaponry.

   A CTBT would contribute significantly to the stabilization of the non-proliferation regime. It would demand real sacrifices from nuclear weapon states and lay down obligations in a non-discriminatory way. Nuclear threshold states would be exposed to considerable international pressure to join such a treaty. A new barrier for using the nuclear option would therefore be erected. That a CTBT is not beyond reach is shown by the nearly successful negotiations in the late 1970s.

58. Admittedly there are still many obstacles in the way of such a treaty. Verification and the ageing of the nuclear weapons stockpiles are often quoted. Both problems are real, but they do not appear to pose insurmountable barriers if the political will exists to achieve an agreement.

   It will not be easy to achieve a European consensus on this issue. Yet those difficulties should not prevent the reconvening of the tripartite negotiations among the UK, the US, and the USSR; this would indicate a new and broader approach to nuclear arms control. If France could be persuaded to join the talks at some point, the signals would become even stronger.

As an interim step the nuclear weapon states could ratify the as yet unratified Threshold Test Ban Treaty of 1974 and agree to negotiate another such treaty to lower the threshold further. In the context of ongoing and promising CTBT negotiations, this would serve as an indicator of serious intent to move to an adequately verifiable CTBT.

59. A significant reduction of the nuclear weapons stockpiles of the US and the USSR would not only satisfy demands of many non-nuclear weapon states, it would also greatly facilitate the active participation of the West European nuclear weapon states in future arms control talks.

If nuclear non-proliferation is to be upheld as a viable policy goal of Western Europe, political sacrifices will be required from European nuclear weapon states. As their nuclear arsenals undergo considerable modernization in quantitative and qualitative terms, they gain real significance in the global nuclear balance. However, they will still be of a lesser magnitude than those of the superpowers.

60. Nevertheless, the creation of an arms control forum in which all five nuclear weapon states could participate would strengthen the non-proliferation regime, even if the smaller arsenals were not yet the subject of concrete negotiations. In this respect, the 1979 accession of France to the UN Committee on Disarmament was a helpful step.

A meeting of all five nuclear weapon states — as proposed by the heads of government of Sweden, Greece, India, Tanzania, Canada, and Argentina (the "Four-Continent Initiative") and also envisaged by the French President — would be a highly visible event. Such a meeting could be useful in setting an agenda for negotiations to be conducted in other forums. It would symbolize the willingness of all nuclear weapon states to commit themselves to arms control, even if the timetables for their entrance into concrete negotiations varied.

61. Western Europe has relied heavily on nuclear weapons for deterrence and for possible defence. Those weapons are being deployed partly on the territory of non-nuclear weapon states. While nuclear deployments are viewed as a strategic necessity by the Western Alliance, they may render the non-proliferation

posture of Western Europe less credible in the eyes of third parties.

Strategy cannot be changed overnight and depends on many more aspects of security policy than non-proliferation alone. But among those considerations, the non-proliferation perspective should properly be taken into account.

The emerging NATO consensus on raising the nuclear threshold is therefore highly commendable. The removal of 1,000 nuclear warheads after the double-track decision of 1979, and the planned removal of another 1,400, point visibly in the direction of a defence strategy that relies less on nuclear war-fighting with short-range battlefield weapons. This is a signal of great importance for the non-proliferation regime. Reducing the emphasis on nuclear weapons for deterrence and defence in Western Europe would strengthen the norm of non-proliferation.

VII. Deterring proliferation actions

62. West European countries, due to their own history, probably have more empathy and understanding of the interests and perceptions of most threshold countries than either superpower. But understanding alone is not sufficient to influence the decisions of those countries in critical situations. A certain degree of leverage is needed if West European countries are to contribute to strengthening existing barriers to further proliferation actions. Leverage exists if relations with Western Europe are valued highly by the threshold countries and if the prospect for endangering those relations by proliferation steps is sufficiently credible.

63. The leading position of West European countries as suppliers of nuclear facilities and materials on the world market gives them a limited yet significant leverage.

    Neither the long recession of the nuclear industry nor the partial and small-scale (but increasing) self-sufficiency of major third world countries should lead to an underrating of this leverage.

    As in the past, if a country wants commercial-scale nuclear imports from a source other than the superpowers in the near future, it will have to turn towards Europe. While nuclear trade is a two-way street, countries interested in major nuclear energy development will hesitate to destroy European good faith in the peaceful character of their programmes.

64. Besides the nuclear field, economic relations with Western Europe are very attractive to threshold countries and other third world nations. Europe provides technology and goods and offers export markets; it is a major source for bilateral and multilateral aid; it has a major voice in international lending institutions. European banks, with the backing of governments, are among the main sources of commercial credit.

    Again, the relationship is one of interdependence. rather than dependence. But, excepting very few cases, the relative importance of the relationship is greater for third world countries than for Europe because of the different sizes of the economies. If it were discreetly yet credibly conveyed that certain proliferation actions would imply reconsideration of the full economic relationship, this could provide a major barrier for any such decision.

65. Foreign relations of the West European countries and the Community as a whole cover more than economic affairs. Regional groupings around the world as well as individual countries are looking for political support.

   Sometimes this means opening an alternative to the superpowers, as in the case of Latin America. Sometimes it means general endorsement for still fragile regional frameworks, as in the case of the recently founded South Asian Regional Cooperation (SARC) development organization. Occasionally very specific support is sought, e.g. South Africa's dependence on a veto against UN Security Council sanctions, or Israel's need for help against expulsion from different international organizations.

   While it is obvious that severing political relations is part of general foreign policy and involves more than just nonproliferation, the mere possibility of adverse change possesses a certain inherent deterrence value.

66. West European countries have emerged as major armaments suppliers. Their exports include everything from simple police weapons to the most sophisticated modern equipment.

   While Europe's role in defence equipment sales can be viewed with mixed feelings, it is very relevant in terms of nonproliferation. For those third world states concerned with security, the steady flow of conventional arms is a major interest. The military establishment would rarely exchange this supply for first generation nuclear forces.

   This interest gives West European governments additional leverage for deterring significant steps towards nuclear weapons, particularly with those countries which now buy arms in Western Europe and which will continue to do so. However, large states equipped with sophisticated conventional weaponry may stimulate their less wealthy opponents to be interested in nuclear weapons.

67. Hence Europe is not without leverage with respect to nuclear proliferation. How and when to use this leverage, however, is an entirely different problem. The analysis above has shown that some countries may perceive it to be in their legitimate national interest to keep a nuclear weapons option open. Attempts to force them to close that option seem unpromising. When highly valued national interests are at stake, the leverage may be too limited to produce the desired results; once expended, the "leverage currency" loses its value rapidly.

The most promising approach is through "normal" diplomacy: continuously conveying West European interest in non-proliferation through the use of cooperative, friendly relations with regional groupings and individual countries. This path is most promising because it can help to shape a future non-proliferation regime of cooperative management.

68. This approach may not always be sufficient to deal with threshold countries strongly inclined towards a nuclear weapons option. In those cases, Europe must make prudent use of both her assets: her good understanding of the situation of those countries and her leverage. *It is probably far more useful to embark on a policy of deterring (from testing and from weapons development) rather than on one of compelling (trying to enforce a basic change of nuclear policy).*

69. Whether this kind of deterrence works largely depends on the credibility of West European reactions to acts of proliferation, e.g. diversion of fissionable materials from civilian activities, breach of contractual obligations, testing a nuclear device, and conducting a test series.

Experience shows that it is difficult to unite many countries behind an effective sanctions policy. In Western Europe, the EC members are probably in the best position to overcome these difficulties due to their institutional interconnections. At least once in the past — during the Falklands (Malvinas) war — they have applied sanctions to a third party, however reluctantly.

Enhancing credibility is another reason why the declaration on non-proliferation by EC heads of government (§ 36) should express strong reservations about additional countries testing a nuclear device and hint at the consequences. The same position should be expressed discreetly and unobtrusively during the conduct of bilateral diplomacy.

VIII. Dealing with specific cases

70. When India exploded a "peaceful" nuclear device in 1974, soon after the first oil crisis, there were again (as in the late 1950s) predictions of run-away nuclear proliferation as a consequence of rapidly expanding nuclear trade. Yet today the problem regions remain the same: nuclear trade has not expanded as expected. New threshold states will probably not approach a nuclear weapons option for at least another decade. This time-gap permits a careful treatment of the existing cases.

While the non-proliferation policy principles outlined above can help to erect barriers and thresholds for further proliferation steps in all those countries, each case differs and must be dealt with separately. No general, uniform prescription can be proposed.

South Asia

71. In South Asia the balance is very delicate. India wants to claim a position as a major regional power and to signal China that a minimum deterrence exists. Pakistan feels a pressing need to catch up with India, which in turn regards the Pakistani nuclear programme with great apprehension. A test by either country or a major conventional contest could lead to a nuclear arms race in South Asia. This is why both nations probably prefer the status quo.

72. A nuclear arms race would be risky and expensive. It would severely drain already scarce resources from development and from conventional armament. If a nuclear arms race began, it is highly likely that Pakistan would lose its arms supplies from the US and lose the race with India. India would have to fear the loss of at least some international aid and political support. Moreover, India has no apparent incentive to conduct further testing at this point in time.

On the other hand, both countries appear to consider it in their national interests to keep a nuclear weapons option open. If the option were taken away, India might perceive it as a serious loss of security and a serious blow to national independence and dignity. Pakistan will follow as long as India keeps the option open.

73. Public statements about nuclear-weapon-free zones and pro-posals for mutual inspection notwithstanding, this will also be

the case in the future. Thus a significant *rapprochement* towards the non-proliferation regime cannot be expected from either state. Pressures on the nuclear sectors of both countries have been unable to change these policies. Indigeneous nuclear technological development is already too high in both countries: access to nuclear weapons materials is available as is the know-how to construct a nuclear explosive. Little can be done from outside to constrain those capabilities.

74. West European influence is necessarily very limited. The French supply of fuel for India's Tarapur reactor yields some influence. But leverage resulting from nuclear relations is really a two-way street in this case because the continuous application of safeguards to Tarapur and the plutonium produced there depends on the delivery of this fuel. Western Europe has no nuclear relationship with Pakistan at present.

This situation could only change if European companies took up the Pakistani request for bids for a Pressurized Water Reactor (PWR) or if India asked for bids for PWRs in order to reach its goal of 10,000 MW nuclear electrical capacity by the year 2000. Whether renewed nuclear trade would be viewed as surrender to South Asian nuclear option policies or yield a certain leverage is open to question. Neither nation depends on nuclear energy for more than 10% of its power generation at present; despite ambitious programmes, this situation will only change slowly over the next decade.

Thus this leverage, if it existed, would be severely constrained and unusable if a national emergency arose for either country. In addition, the leverage could only be acquired if there were no request for full-scope safeguards attached to the renewed trade.

75. West European countries *can* marginally add to existing barriers and thereby shift the precarious balance between incentives and disincentives slightly in favour of preserving the status quo. This must be done very carefully lest the Pakistanis feel even more cornered and the Indians more tempted to defy what they perceive as a policy of domination.

West European satisfaction with the "no-test" state since 1974 should be expressed in diplomatic exchanges with both parties. Any heavy-handed pursuit of non-proliferation policy would be unwise and counterproductive in a situation of precarious political stability and strong national sensitivities.

76. Beyond that, Western Europe could try to give favourable treatment to SARC (South Asian Regional Cooperation, in which both India and Pakistan participate) in order to foster *rapprochement* on the sub-continent over the longer term. The UK could also consider acting as a mediator for Pakistan's re-admittance to the Commonwealth organization.

Joint nuclear projects with Indian as well as Pakistani cooperation (as have already been conducted by the IAEA) should be encouraged. In addition, because the growing rivalry of the Soviet Union and the US in the region has a negative effect on the security perceptions of those countries, attempts should be made to persuade the superpowers to de-emphasize their armed competition in the Indian Ocean region.

Fostering a climate of *détente* and *rapprochement* in the region should be on the agenda whenever European states, individually or in common, consider their policy towards South Asia.

77. But there should be no illusions: the key to non-proliferation in the region lies with India and Pakistan themselves. Development of a finely tuned regional hierarchy in which each country accepts a certain position *vis-à-vis* its superior rival — India *vis-à-vis* China, Pakistan *vis-à-vis* India — cannot be imposed from outside. It is up to India and Pakistan to find a way to live with the present status quo, which seems to be more in their mutual interest than a nuclear arms race. Western Europe should not miss opportunitites to contribute to a cooperative climate, but such actions certainly cannot substitute for decisions of the South Asian countries themselves.

Middle East

78. The Middle Eastern situation is extremely different. On one side are the Arab states and Iran — some of which have signalled some motivation for acquiring nuclear weapons but may still lack the capability for the next 15 years. On the other side is Israel, with the reputation of already possessing a small number of first generation nuclear weapons and with no visible need for a nuclear test or an open nuclear strategy.

79. The Israeli desire for a deterrence of last resort derives from the country's dangerous geopolitical situation. This situation has been improved by the Camp David Agreement with Egypt and the impressive superiority of Israeli weapons in conventional encounters in the Middle East. Thus there is no pressing need for Israel to change its present position.

The events which would force Israel towards an open nuclear deterrent strategy — an Arab state acquiring nuclear weapons, Arab conventional superiority, or massive Soviet involvement in the Middle East — all appear remote at present. But because none is fully inconceivable either, Israel will preserve its option. Short of those events, Israel will try to avoid the strains on its relationship with the US and Western Europe, and the enormous pressure on Arab leaders to react accordingly, which an open Israeli nuclear posture would entail. Disincentives are certainly stronger than incentives at present.

80. On the Arab side, Iraq and Libya have given ambiguous signals concerning their nuclear intentions even though they are parties to the NPT. Both are in a very early stage of nuclear development and lack the industrial infrastructure needed to support a large indigenous programme. To bring them up to nuclear weapons capability may require 15 years or more of undisturbed nuclear research.

Iran, a major non-Arab player in the Middle East conflict and suspect for its erratic foreign policy, might have been in a more advanced position. But the country's nuclear establishment was disrupted by the revolution and is hard to rebuild. Therefore Iran is possibly as far away from a nuclear bomb as Libya and Iraq.

81. The other Arab countries, particularly Syria and Egypt, have been extremely careful not to excite Israel's fears and suspicions in the nuclear field (which erupted so violently in the bombardment of the Osiraq reactor). Painfully aware of the escalation risks, both have avoided reacting to the alleged Israeli nuclear weapon with programmes of their own, which could have fed Israeli suspicions. They have ratified the NPT and have given clear indications that they do not plan to go into sensitive activities for the time being. Given the state of their nuclear programmes, it would also take Egypt and Syria 15 years or more to come close to a nuclear weapon.

82. The most likely scenario, therefore, is one in which Israel keeps its option open while the Arabs and Iran drift very slowly to higher levels of nuclear capability. If that time can be used to foster a major Arab-Israeli *rapprochement*, then a nuclear-weapon-free zone in the Middle East — which at present has little chance of realization — would become a more serious possibility.

Despite much discussion, nuclear proliferation remains a dormant issue in the Middle East. Thus non-proliferation policies for this region must be careful not to dramatize unnecessarily this relatively comfortable situation.

83. The Middle East is a region where supply policies can have a marked influence on the situation. There should be no nuclear exports to Israel. Given its very equivocal position towards non-proliferation and safeguards and its defiance of the non-proliferation regime expressed by the raid on Osiraq, such exports would put serious doubts on the credibility of the regime.

For the rest of the Middle East, restraint should be the rule. In principle, no sensitive equipment should be supplied. The risk of provoking violent reactions is just too great. The utmost restraint should be exercised before supplying new nuclear equipment to Iran and Iraq while the war continues, and to Libya until it demonstrates a marked shift from its past erratic foreign policy and puts an end to support for terrorism. The principle that nuclear exports be tailored to real needs should be observed strictly. The policy of restraint will no doubt be helped by the weak demand for nuclear energy to be expected from this region.

84. It should be explained to Israel that any action towards an open nuclear posture, except for extreme circumstances, would oblige Europe to reconsider their economic relationship. While the termination of the EC-Israeli economic cooperation agreement poses difficult legal problems, the severing of economic relations is a certain disincentive in Israeli eyes.

Beyond that, opportunities for a West European non-proliferation policy in the Middle East are severely constrained. US difficulties of promoting Middle East peace have shown the intrinsic problems of attempts to pacify the region from outside. European countries should be prepared to offer their diplomatic services (e.g. for mediation) and to participate in peace-keeping operations. However the impact of such activities on non-proliferation is limited.

South Africa

85. In South Africa, the external situation has somewhat stabilized during the past five years. Deep fears within the white population of a "total onslaught" have given way to a greater feeling of external security. The development of a nuclear weapon — once viewed as possible in the context of a "total strategy" — may be less attractive today. Recent events have proved the conventional superiority of South African armed forces over those of neighbouring states.

Nuclear weapons are of no use in the activities of the South African military forces: policing domestic guerilla warfare and conducting ambush actions against the front-line states. There is no visible incentive for exploding a nuclear device or developing nuclear weapons. Events which would change the situation dramatically — an African state approaching the nuclear weapons threshold, a sudden improvement in the front states' military capabilities, or a massive Soviet commitment to southern Africa — are all highly improbable. The Soviet Union has observed events in the region with utmost restraint; the possibility of a Soviet threat appears extremely remote.

86. On the other hand, no significant improvement of South Africa's non-proliferation stance is to be expected. The two Koeberg power reactors are subject to IAEA safeguards. In addition, the government has taken an important step by publicizing its adherence to the London Guidelines and by voluntarily seeking a safeguards agreement on its commerical enrichment plant. To do the same with the unsafeguarded pilot enrichment plant, or even to accede to the NPT, would deprive South Africa of what it may perceive as useful bargaining chips in its dealings with the West. Given the country's delicate situation, and particularly its isolation, it is unlikely that it would give up these trump cards lightly.

87. Nor is there an incentive that the West is able or willing to offer which would be tempting enough for the South African government to change its position. The three rewards which South Africa would certainly value highly — public diplomatic support for its regional order policy, an end to the arms embargo, and restoration of its position in the IAEA — are out of the question for political reasons.

Nuclear cooperation holds little promise. South Africa will be in a position to supply its own fuel for the Koeberg reactors and the South African economy would probably survive through the end of the century without additional nuclear power plants, even though there are indications that the government has plans to build still more plants.

Leverage is also limited. Because South Africa has already manoeuvred itself into isolation, it does not have too much to lose. The threat it earnestly fears is the application of full-fledged economic sanctions by the UN Security Council. For protection against this it relies on the vetos of the West's permanent members. Such sanctions are not likely, nor would they realistically bring South Africa closer to the non-proliferation regime. The threat is more credible as a deterrence to South Africa testing a bomb.

88. When joint diplomatic activities by European countries, the US, and Canada successfully prevented a South African nuclear test in 1977 (the so-called Kalahari incident), it showed that the West has at least some influence on South African nuclear decisions.

Although economic sanctions impose a certain cost on Western Europe, the political cost of *not* reacting to a South African nuclear explosion would probably be higher. In such a case, Europe could not stand idle without provoking the wrath of even the most pro-West black African leaders. The lack of a Western response might reopen broad inroads for the Soviet Union to the heart of black Africa. There would also be strong pressures for resolute reaction within some European countries because of public opposition to apartheid policy. It should be made clear to the South African government, through available political channels, that a nuclear test would have grave consequences for its relations with Western Europe.

One must also recognize that the case of South Africa presents particular difficulties. There is a potential conflict between those policies that might move South Africa closer to the regime and those that many Western Europeans consider essential in the light of South Africa's racial policies.

89. In the longer term, if the security environment remains as it is or even improves, and if the safeguarding of the commercial enrichment plant follows a satisfactory course, it is not totally inconceivable that South Africa would also accept safeguards on its pilot plant. This would still leave signing of the NPT as a bargaining chip, but would temper proliferation accusations and fears. Such considerations should be raised and encouraged through prudent diplomacy.

Thus in the case of South Africa, incentives to further proliferation are quite low while disincentives are considerable. Europe has no opportunities to improve the status quo. But it has limited leverage to prevent it from becoming worse.

South America

90. South America has always been thought the least pressing non-proliferation case because of the lack of serious security problems related to nuclear weapons. The Falklands (Malvinas) war administered a shock to Latin American perceptions of

strategies and needs. On the other hand, changes in governments in Argentina and Brazil may have modified their interest in military usage of nuclear energy. There are some indications of a small, separate, military-directed nuclear programme in Brazil which could become a source for concern in the future despite its relatively small budget. If this proved true, the positive trend on the Argentinian side may be reversed.

91. The motivations in both countries present a very specific mix of security concerns and status aspirations. Many in Brazil view their country as a major power which deserves a seat among the great nations of the world. A nuclear capability might be thought to underline this claim. The nuclear option is also seen as a possible deterrence to outside incursions into the Brazilian sphere of influence.

It would be hard for Argentina to accept inferior status, although it cannot match Brazilian strength in terms of population, size, and raw materials. The nuclear field is the single area where Argentina is clearly ahead of its neighbour and the Argentinians have for a long while been determined to keep this advantage — a posture hardly acceptable to Brazil in the long run.

In reacting to the South Atlantic conflict, the Argentinians have as yet only hinted at the possibility of producing nuclear-propelled submarines and have protested over the UK's alleged introduction of nuclear weapons in waters claimed to be covered by the Tlatelolco Treaty. How long such a restrained posture will continue must be measured in part by the success of any negotiation between the UK and Argentina on the future of the Falkland Islands.

92. The most important change in both countries is the move from military to civilian rule. But Argentina still has to struggle with the consequences of military rule. The relations between the civilian government and the armed forces are difficult and precarious. A sudden change of nuclear policy is perhaps too great a risk as long as the stability of civilian rule is not assured.

The impact of political change on the two countries' nuclear programmes is ambiguous. The Argentinian Atomic Energy Commission (AEC) was put under civilian control and suffered severe budget cuts. But the new government reaffirmed the old reservations against ratifying the Tlatelolco Treaty: ambiguity of safeguards and peaceful nuclear explosion (PNE) regulations, unjustified interpretations of the treaty by the US and the USSR, and reactions to the Falklands (Malvinas) war.

93. In South America, as in the other cases, the incentives are not overwhelming. Continued nuclear cooperation with supplier states provides both Argentina and Brazil with a reason not to cross the testing threshold. Brazil is bound by the agreement with the Federal Republic of Germany to put all supplied facilities under safeguards and to do the same with any plant using the same technological processes, even if the technology was acquired domestically or from third parties. This last rule is valid through 1998. It would be difficult for Brazil to produce weapons-grade fissile material in the foreseeable future without breaching the agreement.

Economic leverage should be treated with utmost restraint. All too easily both countries could be pressed into a posture of defiance which is not at all conducive to non-proliferation. Instead, nuclear cooperation in Latin America should be encouraged. This could mean Argentinian ratification of the Tlatelolco Treaty. To achieve this goal, even some ambiguous language concerning PNEs could be tolerated.

An alternative would be an "ABC" solution for South America, i.e., intensified nuclear collaboration among Argentina, Brazil, and Chile. Such collaboration would improve mutual information about the neighbours' nuclear programmes. It might thus serve as a confidence-building arrangement which would reduce incentives for a regional nuclear capability race. The announcement in early 1985 that Argentina and Brazil have agreed in principle on mutual inspection of their nuclear facilities is a very promising step which deserves support.

94. The key to regional pacification is likely to lie in Argentina. For the civilian government, stabilization of the young democracy depends on a precarious balance of domestic politics and foreign policy. Most observers agree that, while there is no direct link between the Argentinian claim to the Falkland Islands (Malvinas) and an Argentinian nuclear weapon, progress on the Falklands (Malvinas) issue might make it easier for the government to deal with domestic public opinion and thereby enhance its leeway for a more positive attitude towards the Tlatelolco Treaty.

In their diplomatic dealings with Brazil, West European countries should bear in mind the importance of status and the emphasis on North-South relations in Brazil's foreign policy. The attitudes of the Brazilian elite towards proliferation will be at least partly influenced through issues which seem very remote from nuclear questions themselves.

Summary

95. In all four regional cases discussed above, it is obvious that any outside influence, and particularly that of Western Europe, remains very limited. Rather than trying to compel the threshold states towards acceptance of far reaching non-proliferation obligations, it is sensible to augment the deterrence effects of the existing balance of incentives and disincentives which presently favours the status quo in all cases. This can be done by a cautious export policy and public endorsement of non-proliferation goals, combined with discreet but audible messages to all countries in question that a change in the status quo cannot but hurt relationships. This is a modest but feasible policy. However, it requires a higher degree of West European coordination than has been achieved so far.

IX. Conclusions

96. In the past fifteen years, a consensus on non-proliferation policy in Western Europe has been developing. This consensus is far from being perfect; many political difficulties remain. Nuclear policies vary widely among West European countries and non-proliferation policy is still the prerogative of the individual nations.

However, a joint European approach would considerably strengthen the existing non-proliferation regime. Increasing coordination among West European countries is therefore needed. Developments so far, and particularly the Working Group on Non-Proliferation within European Political Cooperation, justify hope for further progress.

97. Small incremental improvements of the existing regime hold better promises for success than attempts to achieve dramatic changes. One such step could be a joint declaration on non-proliferation by the EC heads of government. This declaration should stress the interest of West European countries in non-proliferation and their opposition to testing by non-nuclear weapon states. Progress on arms control — particularly a Test Ban Treaty coupled with "build downs" of strategic and theatre nuclear weapon systems — would make a unique contribution to the preservation of the legitimacy of the regime. Policies seeking less reliance on nuclear weapons for national and alliance security are also important. Another major task for the future is the integration of new suppliers into the regime.

98. Prudent export policy remains an integral part of non-proliferation policy. It must find a middle ground between strict denial and export promotion. The London Guidelines provide a solid base. The next step should be the development of a pragmatic code of conduct — within the framework of the Guidelines — for dealing with export problems on a case-by-case basis. This code should give proper attention to the sensitivity of the items to be exported as well as to recipients' records.

99. In the foreseeable future, proliferation concerns will focus on a small number of countries. Most of those threshold countries have made great progress in indigenous nuclear technological capabilities. Whether they will use these capabilities for military applications will depend on their assessments of their national interests. Working through the balance of incentives and disincentives as perceived by the threshold countries will in most instances offer the best prospects for success. Preserving

the status quo of no further testing through careful diplomatic efforts is the most promising approach towards these countries.

100. In shaping non-proliferation policy, two important aspects should be borne in mind: the inevitable limits of this policy and the relation of nuclear proliferation to broader issues of international politics. The limits derive from our international system of sovereign nation-states and apply to both the general non-proliferation regime and the possible influence on individual states.

- In the absence of world government, any non-proliferation regime is bound to be imperfect. To consolidate, build on, and seek wider acceptance of the gains made so far is the wisest course today.

- The decisions of governments in the field of security follow their assessments of national interest. This restricts the opportunity for shaping these decisions from outside.

It is essential to temper expectations in both respects. Expectations that are too high may lead to frustration and over-reactions. Non-proliferation policy needs continuity and predictability.

101. Nuclear proliferation is related to, and partly dependent on, broader issues of international relations. Further development of the North-South dialogue will have a strong impact on the general climate for preserving and improving the non-proliferation regime. The evolution of the East-West conflict influences the security of some key threshold states and determines the chances for meaningful arms control, which again has consequences for the non-proliferation regime. This evolution also affects the standards of international behaviour and the means chosen to influence security relations. Many actions in the arena of foreign policy therefore have intentional or unintentional effects on nuclear proliferation.

102. Finally, non-proliferation would benefit from further progress in the difficult process of West European political integration. A very important aspect of this process is the coordination of security policies, including arms control. A joint approach towards non-proliferation would necessarily be a relevant ingredient of such a unified security policy.

Taken together, our considerations suggest that West Europeans can make a significant contribution to non-proliferation policy. They should not miss the opportunity.

Appendixes

Appendix A: A comparison
of the two reports*

The parallel studies whose conclusions are summarized in this volume grew out of a conviction, based on the record of international non-proliferation policies in the 1970s, that no single country can curb the spread of nuclear weapons alone. Past U.S.-European quarrels over non-proliferation were a source of weakness in the non-proliferation regime. Thus one purpose of creating the two separate panels—whose membership included a number of persons who have held or still hold relevant government positions—was to provide an indication of the prospects and basis for a common Atlantic approach that was realistically possible. As shown below, the reports reveal a surprising degree of consensus between the two groups.

But attention is first called to a crucial prior question, which the project was also designed to explore: to what degree the West Europeans themselves would be capable of speaking with one voice in this field. The European panel consisted of nationals from seven sovereign states (and an official of the European Commission, a body with fairly limited "federal" authority). For the Europeans, agreement meant surmounting the idiosyncracies of political outlook, tradition, and decision-making of their respective countries or organizations. While the U.S. panel was reassessing U.S. policy, on which there had been a wealth of prior U.S. studies, for Western Europe this was the first attempt to produce a report with a specific European view on the issue—a pioneer work whose success was uncertain in the beginning. Thus, it is significant that the European panel succeeded in producing a document dealing with all the critical and often divisive issues without a single reservation and with the signature of all panel participants. This offers hope that with sufficient effort and much goodwill, the West European countries may be capable of establishing a common non-proliferation policy.

In comparing the two summary reports, one is struck by the extent of agreement between the U.S. and West European groups both at the more general, "philosophical," level and on more specific issues.

As for the "philosophy": First, both reports refrain from an alarmist attitude. The non-proliferation problem calls for sensible, thoughtful and resolute action, but not for doomsday panic. Second, both reports emphasize the limits even a coordinated non-proliferation policy faces *vis-à-vis* countries pursuing their own perceived national interests. Within those limits both panels feel non-proliferation policy still has a fair chance of success, particularly since the net advantages of acquiring nuclear weapons are far from clear. Third, both agree that diplomacy has to play a far greater role,

---

* Based on materials prepared by the Rapporteurs of the respective reports.

and technical approaches a more limited one. This poses greater challenges to the politicians, since it means moving the issue up in the hierarchy of foreign policy concerns and integrating it firmly into everyday diplomatic activities. Fourth, agreement exists on the delicate balance between cooperative and threat/punitive elements of the policy. It should be biased towards the first, the collaborative component. Threat and punishment ought to be reserved for the most serious and extreme cases in highly circumscribed circumstances. As a universalized approach, they not only create resentment, but their currency gets quickly depreciated.

A more detailed comparison of the two reports shows that: Both reports focus on (1) preserving the present widespread consensus and commitments against further proliferation, and (2) averting further proliferatory steps by certain states of special current concern. Both call for fuller recognition of the impact on these objectives of how related issues of foreign policy, nuclear doctrine and posture, and nuclear arms control are handled. Both point to the need for approaches that can adapt to technical and political change and help contain more advanced stages of proliferation. Both discuss the significant contribution that a comprehensive test ban treaty could make to non-proliferation if other current obstacles to its achievement could be overcome. (The European panel suggests a first step towards breaking the present stalemate.) And both briefly address the problem of coping with nuclear risks posed by terrorist or other subnational groups.

In some respects, the two reports are complementary. Thus, for example, the U.S. report discusses the limited relevance of U.S. non-proliferation legislation to the cases of greatest current concern, while the European report notes the reaction of the West European countries to that legislation. The European report focuses on the special role that the West European countries could play in containing further proliferation, discusses their potential leverage and the progress they have made in evolving a consensus on the subject, and suggests ways in which the coordination of European policies in this field could be improved. The U.S. report, while stressing the need for more active involvement by non-nuclear weapon states, also discusses the utility of cooperation with the Soviet Union in this field. The European report gives somewhat fuller treatment to the pertinence of progress in nuclear arms control and deemphasizing nuclear weapons, and to ways of strengthening support for the International Atomic Energy Agency; while the U.S. report says more about sanctions, positive and negative security assurances, and ways of avoiding regional competition in the development of nuclear explosives for "peaceful" purposes.

As noted above, these reports indicate far more agreement than disagreement between the two groups, both in their assessment of the current situation and in their recommendations for containing it.

In discussing the six states of greatest current concern (Pakistan, India, Israel, South Africa, Argentina, and Brazil) both reports cite the growing capabilities of these countries, but express guarded optimism that dramatic changes in the present situation—such as initiation of a series of weapons tests—can be averted at least for the next several years. They emphasize that the decision depends upon these governments' assessment of their own national interests, which may be influenced but cannot be dictated by others. But they suggest that, at least in the near term, these governments are more likely to see the disadvantages of such dramatic changes as outweighing the advantages. The challenge is to reenforce this balance of considerations against further proliferatory action. The U.S. report identifies some of the considerations that should be weighed by such governments in making those assessments, while noting that these points would be more persuasive if presented by non-nuclear weapon states. It also stresses the pertinence of efforts to reduce underlying regional tensions, and proposes some specific non-proliferation goals and approaches for each of these countries. The European report points to the limited, yet widely unused diplomatic assets of Western Europe for this purpose.*

On preserving the existing international non-proliferation regime, both reports point out the need to begin laying the groundwork for extension of the Non-Proliferation Treaty beyond 1995, and note the importance of further efforts to reap the full benefits of the Treaty for the Prohibition of Nuclear Weapons in Latin America (the Treaty of Tlatelolco). And both find stronger, uninterrupted support of the International Atomic Energy Agency indispensable.

The strongest divergence exists on nuclear export policy, though both reports at least endorse the Nuclear Suppliers' Guidelines (originally adopted in 1976 by major supplier countries and subsequently joined by others, including all other members of the European Communities in 1984). The U.S. report urges that nuclear supplier countries adopt, as a condition of any significant new nuclear supply commitments to non-nuclear weapon states, a requirement that the recipient country accept safeguards on all of its peaceful nuclear activities. The European report, while endorsing that objective and recognizing the dilemma posed by merely partial safeguards in an importing country, suggests that where it is clear that an importer will not accept this condition and where the export does not involve particularly sensitive items, it may be better to settle for the closest achievable equivalent than to risk nuclear autarky. This conclusion was also based on concern about how to draw into the regime new suppliers with a capability to undercut the regime, and to keep at least parts of national programs under safeguards.

Both agree on the need for "restraint" in the export of weapons-usable materials or uranium enrichment or chemical reprocessing equipment or technology, but also see a need for some differentiation among cases. Both

---

* The most striking difference on this aspect of the problem relates to the policy towards the Middle East. Western Europe feels far less politically inhibited from dealing with Israel on the nuclear issue but lacks the leverage. The United States, with strong leverage, is virtually incapable of acting due to political impediments.

suggest, as factors to be taken into account in making such differentiation, the extent to which the proposed recipient country already has access to weapons-usable materials; the economic justification for the import;* whether the proposed recipient country has agreed to accept safeguards on all its peaceful nuclear activities and otherwise demonstrated its commitment to avoiding proliferation; and the volatility of the region in which it is located.

At the start of its deliberations, the U.S. panel looked closely at the potential utility of economic sanctions as a deterrent or response to acts of proliferation. Its report points out some of the limitations of this approach and warns against overestimating its efficacy. The European report reaches a similarly cautious conclusion. Nevertheless, both note that a failure to mount a significant response to clear violations of safeguards or non-proliferation commitments, or to a nuclear detonation by a non-nuclear weapon state, would undermine the non-proliferation regime, and recommend consultations among concerned supplier countries to plan and coordinate such response.

* The Europeans would apply this criterion only to politically sensitive cases.

Appendix B: Treaty on the Non-Proliferation of Nuclear Weapons

Parties to the treaty as of 1 September 1985

Treaty on the Non-Proliferation of Nuclear Weapons

Signed at London, Moscow, and Washington 1 July 1968; entered into force 5 March 1970

The States concluding this Treaty, hereinafter referred to as the "Parties to the Treaty,"

Considering the devastation that would be visited upon all mankind by a nuclear war and the consequent need to make every effort to avert the danger of such a war and to take measures to safeguard the security of peoples,

Believing that the proliferation of nuclear weapons would seriously enhance the danger of nuclear war,

In conformity with resolutions of the United Nations General Assembly calling for the conclusion of an agreement on the prevention of wider dissemination of nuclear weapons,

Undertaking to cooperate in facilitating the application of International Atomic Energy Agency safeguards on peaceful nuclear activities,

Expressing their support for research, development and other efforts to further the application, within the framework of the International Atomic Energy Agency safeguards system, of the principle of safeguarding effectively the flow of source and special fissionable materials by use of instruments and other techniques at certain strategic points,

Affirming the principle that the benefits of peaceful applications of nuclear technology, including any technological by-products which may be derived by nuclear-weapon States from the development of nuclear explosive devices, should be available for peaceful purposes to all Parties to the Treaty, whether nuclear-weapon or non-nuclear weapon States,

Convinced that, in furtherance of this principle, all Parties to the Treaty are entitled to participate in the fullest possible exchange of scientific information for, and to contribute alone or in cooperation with other States to, the further development of the applications of atomic energy for peaceful purposes,

Declaring their intention to achieve at the earliest possible date the cessation of the nuclear arms race and to undertake effective measures in the direction of nuclear disarmament,

Urging the cooperation of all States in the attainment of this objective,

Recalling the determination expressed by the Parties to the 1963 Treaty banning nuclear weapon tests in the atmosphere in outer space and under water in its Preamble to seek to achieve the discontinuance of all test explosions of nuclear weapons for all time and to continue negotiations to this end,

Desiring to further the easing of international tension and the strengthening of trust between States in order to facilitate the cessation of the manufacture of nuclear weapons, the liquidation of all their existing stockpiles, and the elimination from national arsenals of nuclear weapons and the means of their delivery pursuant to a treaty on general and complete disarmament under strict and effective international control,

Recalling that, in accordance with the Charter of the United Nations, States must refrain in their international relations from the threat or use of force against the territorial integrity or political independence of any State, or in any other manner inconsistent with the Purposes of the United Nations, and that the establishment and maintenance of international peace and security are to be promoted with the least diversion for armaments of the world's human and economic resources,

Have agreed as follows:

Article I

Each nuclear-weapon State Party to the Treaty undertakes not to transfer to any recipient whatsoever nuclear weapons or other nuclear explosive devices or control over such weapons or explosive devices directly, or indirectly; and not in any way to assist, encourage, or induce any non-nuclear-weapon State to manufacture or otherwise acquire nuclear weapons or other nuclear explosive devices, or control over such weapons or explosive devices.

Article II

Each non-nuclear-weapon State Party to the Treaty undertakes not to receive the transfer from any transferor whatsoever of nuclear weapons or other nuclear explosives or of control over such weapons or explosive devices directly, or indirectly; nor to manufacture or otherwise acquire nuclear weapons or other nuclear explosive devices; and not to seek or receive any assistance in the manufacture of nuclear weapons or other nuclear explosive devices.

Article III

1. Each non-nuclear-weapon State Party to the Treaty undertakes to accept safeguards, as set forth in an agreement to be negotiated and concluded with the International Atomic Energy Agency in accordance with the Statute of the International Atomic Energy Agency and the Agency's safeguards system for the exclusive purpose of verification of the fulfillment of its obligations assumed under this Treaty with a view to preventing diversion of nuclear energy from peaceful uses to nuclear

weapons or other nuclear explosive devices. Procedures for the safeguards required by this article shall be followed with respect to source or special fissionable material whether it is being produced, processed or used in any principal nuclear facility or is outside any such facility. The safeguards required by this article shall be applied on all source or special fissionable material in all peaceful nuclear activities within the territory of such State, under its jurisdiction, or carried out under its control anywhere.

2. Each State Party to the Treaty undertakes not to provide: (a) source or special fissionable material, or (b) equipment or material especially designed or prepared for the processing, use or production of special fissionable material, to any non-nuclear-weapon State for peaceful purposes, unless the source or special fissionable material shall be subject to the safeguards required by this article.

3. The safeguards required by this article shall be implemented in a manner designed to comply with article IV of this Treaty, and to avoid hampering the economic or technological development of the Parties or international cooperation in the field of peaceful nuclear activities, including the international exchange of nuclear material and equipment for the processing, use or production of nuclear material for peaceful purposes in accordance with the provisions of this article and the principle of safeguarding set forth in the Preamble of the Treaty.

4. Non-nuclear-weapon States Party to the Treaty shall conclude agreements with the International Atomic Energy Agency to meet the requirements of this article either individually or together with other States in accordance with the Statute of the International Atomic Energy Agency. Negotiation of such agreements shall commence within 180 days from the original entry into force of this Treaty. For States depositing their instruments of ratification or accession after the 180-day period, negotiation of such agreements shall commence not later than the date of such a deposit. Such agreements shall enter into force not later than eighteen months after the date of initiation of negotiations.

Article IV

1. Nothing in this Treaty shall be interpreted as affecting the inalienable right of all the Parties to the Treaty to develop research, production and use of nuclear energy for peaceful purposes without discrimination and in conformity with articles I and II of this Treaty.

2. All the Parties to the Treaty undertake to facilitate, and have the right to participate in, the fullest possible exchange of equipment, materials and scientific and technological information for the peaceful uses of nuclear energy. Parties to the Treaty in a position to do so shall also cooperate in contributing alone or together with other States or international organizations to the further development of the applications of nuclear energy for peaceful purposes, especially in the territories of non-nuclear-weapon States Party to the Treaty, with due consideration for the needs of the developing areas of the world.

Article V

Each Party to the Treaty undertakes to take appropriate measures to ensure that, in accordance with this Treaty, under appropriate international observation and through appropriate international procedures, potential benefits from any peaceful applications of nuclear explosions will be made available to non-nuclear-weapon States Party to the Treaty on a non-discriminatory basis and that the charge to such Parties for the explosive devices used will be as low as possible and exclude any charge for research and development. Non-nuclear-weapon States Party to the Treaty shall be able to obtain such benefits, pursuant to a special international agreement or agreements, through an appropriate international body with adequate representation of non-nuclear-weapon States. Negotiations on this subject shall commence as soon as possible after the Treaty enters into force. Non-nuclear-weapon States Party to the Treaty so desiring may also obtain such benefits pursuant to bilateral agreements.

Article VI

Each of the Parties to the Treaty undertakes to pursue negotiations in good faith on effective measures relating to cessation of the nuclear arms race at an early date and to nuclear disarmament, and on a treaty on general and complete disarmament under strict and effective international control.

Article VII

Nothing in this Treaty affects the right of any group of States to conclude regional treaties in order to assure the total absence of nuclear weapons in their respective territories.

Article VIII

1. Any Party to the Treaty may propose amendments to this Treaty. The text of any proposed amendment shall be submitted to the Depositary Governments which shall circulate it to all Parties to the Treaty. Thereupon, if requested to do so by one-third or more of the Parties to the Treaty, the Depositary Governments shall convene a conference, to which they shall invite all the Parties to the Treaty, to consider such an amendment.

2. Any amendment to this Treaty must be approved by a majority of the votes of all the Parties to the Treaty, including the votes of all nuclear-weapon States to the Treaty and all other Parties which, on the date the amendment is circulated, are members of the Board of Govenors of the International Atomic Energy Agency. The amendment shall enter into force for each Party that deposits its instrument of ratification of the amendment upon the deposit of such intruments of ratification by a majority of all the Parties, including the instruments of ratification of all nuclear-weapon States to the Treaty and all other Parties which, on the date the amendment is circulated, are members of the Board of Govenors of the International Atomic Energy Agency. Thereafter, it shall

enter into force for any other Party upon the deposit of its instrument of ratification of the amendment.

3. Five years after the entry into force of this Treaty, a conference of Parties to the Treaty shall be held in Geneva, Switzerland, in order to review the operation of this Treaty with a view to assuring that the purposes of the Preamble and the provisions of the Treaty are being realized. At intervals of five years thereafter, a majority of the Parties to the Treaty may obtain, by submitting a proposal to this effect to the Depositary Governments, the convening of further conferences with the same objective of reviewing the operation of the Treaty.

Article IX

1. This Treaty shall be open to all States for signature. Any State which does not sign the Treaty before its entry into force in accordance with paragraph 3 of this article may accede to it at any time.

2. This Treaty shall be subject to ratification by signatory States. Instruments of ratification and instruments of accession shall be deposited with the Governments of the United States of America, the United Kingdom of Great Britain and Northern Ireland and the Union of Soviet Socialist Republics, which are hereby designated the Depositary Governments.

3. This Treaty shall enter into force after its ratification by the States, the governments of which are designated Depositaries of the Treaty, and forty other States signatory to this Treaty and the deposit of their instruments of ratification. For the purposes of this Treaty, a nuclear-weapon State is one which has manufactured and exploded a nuclear weapon or other nuclear explosive device prior to January 1, 1967.

4. For States whose instruments of ratification or accession are deposited subsequent to the entry into force of this Treaty, it shall enter into force on the date of the deposit of their instruments of ratification or accession.

5. The Depositary Governments shall promptly inform all signatory and acceding States of the date of each signature, the date of deposit of each instrument of ratification or of accession, the date of the entry into force of this Treaty, and the date of receipt of any requests for convening a conference or other notices.

6. This Treaty shall be registered by the Depositary Governments pursuant to article 102 of the Charter of the United Nations.

Article X

1. Each Party shall in exercising its national sovereignty have the right to withdraw from the Treaty if it decides that extraordinary events, related to the subject matter of this Treaty, have jeopardized the supreme interests of its country. It shall give notice of such withdrawal to all other Parties to the Treaty and to the United Nations Security Council three months in advance. Such notice shall include a statement of the extraordinary events it regards as having jeopardized its supreme interests.

2. Twenty-five years after the entry into force of the Treaty, a conference shall be convened to decide whether the Treaty shall continue in force indefinitely, or shall be extended for an additional fixed period or periods. This decision shall be taken by a majority of the Parties to the Treaty.

Article XI

This Treaty, the English, Russian, French, Spanish and Chinese texts of which are equally authentic, shall be deposited in the archives of the Depositary Governments. Duly certified copies of this Treaty shall be transmitted by the Depositary Governments to the Governments of the signatory and acceding States.

Parties to the NPT as of 1 September 1985

Signed and Ratified or Acceded

Europe

Austria	Greece	Poland
Belgium	Holy See	Portugal
Bulgaria	Hungary	Romania
Cyprus	Iceland	San Marino
Czechoslovakia	Ireland	Sweden
Denmark	Italy	Switzerland
Federal Republic	Liechtenstein	Turkey
of Germany	Luxembourg	USSR
Finland	Malta	United Kingdom
German Democratic	Netherlands	Yugoslavia
Republic	Norway	

Asia and the Pacific

Afghanistan	Korea, Republic of	Philippines
Australia	Laos People's Demo-	Singapore
Bangladesh	cratic Republic	Solomon Islands
Bhutan Brunei	Malaysia	Sri Lanka
Democratic	Maldives	Taiwan
Kampuchea	Mongolia	Thailand
Fiji	Nauru	Tonga
Indonesia	Nepal	Tuvalu
Japan	New Zealand	Viet Nam, Socialist
Kiribati	Papua New Guinea	Republic of
		Western Samoa

Africa and the Middle East

Benin
Botswana
Burkina Faso
Burundi
Cape Verde
Central African
    Republic
Chad
Congo, People's
    Republic
Democratic Yemen
Egypt
Equatorial Guinea
Ethiopia
Gabon
Gambia
Ghana
Guinea

Guinea Bissau
Iran
Iraq
Ivory Coast
Jordan
Kenya
Lebanon
Lesotho
Liberia
Libyan Arab Jama
Madagascar
Mali
Mauritius
Morocco
Nigeria
Rwanda

Sao Tome and
    Principe
Senegal
Seychelles
Sierra Leone
Somalia
Sudan
Swaziland
Syrian Arab Republic
Togo
Tunisia
Uganda
United Republic
    of Cameroon
Zaire

The Americas

Antigua and Barbuda
Bahamas
Barbados
Belize
Bolivia
Canada
Costa Rica
Dominica
Dominican Republic
Ecuador

El Salvador
Grenada
Guatemala
Haiti
Honduras
Jamaica
Mexico
Nicaragua
Panama

Paraguay
Peru
St. Christopher and
    Nevis
St. Lucia
St. Vincent and the
    Grenadines
Surinam
USA
Uruguay
Venezuela

Signed but not ratified

Colombia
Kuwait

Trinidad and Tobago
Yemen Arab Republic

Significant non-parties

France (which has declared, however, that it would behave as if it were a party, and has subscribed to the Nuclear Suppliers' Guidelines

China (which has declared it would require IAEA safeguards on all its nuclear exports to non-nuclear-weapon states)

Spain (all of whose nuclear activities are currently under IAEA safeguards)

Niger (a uranium supplier)

Saudi Arabia (which currently has no nuclear activities)

Argentina	India	Pakistan
Brazil	Israel	South Africa
Cuba		

Note: In December 1985 the Democratic Republic of Korea acceded to the treaty.

Appendix C: Outcome of the 1985 NPT Review Conference*

On September 21, 1985, the 86 parties to the Non-Proliferation Treaty participating in the third quinquennial Review Conference of the Treaty (which included virtually all NPT parties having any significant nuclear activities)[a] adopted by consensus the Final Declaration set forth on the following pages. This result was considerably more positive and constructive than was generally expected and should prove helpful in avoiding defections from the Treaty, winning new parties (such as Spain), and laying the groundwork for extension of the Treaty beyond 1995.

Comparing this document with the two reports included in this volume, we find that:

1. All three bring out the indispensability to an effective non-proliferation regime of the NPT, IAEA safeguards, and uninterrupted support of the IAEA, and the importance of prompt adherence to the Convention on the Physical Protection of Nuclear Materials by all relevant states, though the two panel reports also emphasize other major considerations and complementary approaches.

2. The Declaration deals as follows with the issue of whether comprehensive, full-scope safeguards should be a necessary condition of future supply commitments:

> "The Conference therefore specifically urges all non-nuclear-weapon States not party to the Treaty to make an international legally-binding commitment not to acquire nuclear weapons or other nuclear explosive devices and to accept IAEA safeguards on all their peaceful nuclear activities, both current and future, to verify that commitment. The Conference further urges all states in their international nuclear co-operation and in their nuclear export policies, and specifically as a necessary basis for the transfer of relevant nuclear supplies to non-nuclear-weapon States, to take effective steps towards achieving such a commitment to non-proliferation and acceptance of such safeguards by those States."[b]

While this falls short of the position advocated in the U.S. panel report[c] it

---

* The introductory analysis was prepared by the Rapporteur of the U.S. study.

[a] The only such parties that did not attend were Taiwan and the uranium-exporting states of Gabon and Central African Republic.

[b] Paragraph 4 of review of Article III.

[c] Paragraph 9 of U.S. panel report.

tilts in that direction but seems closer to the position advocated in the European report.[d]

3. The Declaration reflects the high priority given by the overwhelming majority of the parties to prompt resumption of negotiations towards a comprehensive test ban treaty[e] (which is recommended by both panel reports)[f] although it also recognizes the position taken by the present U.S. administration noting that "certain States Party to the Treaty, while committed to the goal of an effectively verifiable comprehensive Nuclear Test Ban Treaty, considered deep and verifiable reductions in existing arsenals of nuclear weapons as the highest priority in the process of pursuing the objective of Article VI [the article of the Treaty that deals with nuclear arms control and disarmament]."[g]

4. The Declaration contains all of the elements of the joint statement on non-proliferation proposed in the European report for issuance by the European Communities[h] although its statement that "any further detonation of a nuclear explosive device by any non-nuclear-weapon state would constitute a serious breach of the non-proliferation objective"[i] is somewhat weaker than recommended in that report or in the corresponding recommendation of the U.S. report.[j]

5. While the Declaration expresses "deep concern that the national nuclear programmes of some States non-Party to the Treaty may lead them to obtain a nuclear weapons capability,"[k] it singles out Israel and South Africa as of special concern,[l] and makes no explicit mention of the other threshold states discussed in the two panel reports, which include a far more detailed analysis of each of the threshold cases.

6. With respect to nuclear export policy (other than safeguards requirements), the Declaration skirts the issue of sensitive nuclear exports discussed in the two panel reports.[m] Apart from safeguards-related recommendations,[n] its recommendation that the IAEA adopt an international

---

[d] Page 44 above and sections 8 and 46–50.

[e] Paragraph 14 of Part B of review of Article VI, as well as the following other parts of the review of that Article: Part A, paragraphs 2, 3, 5, and 14; Part B, paragraphs 5, 6, and 16.

[f] Section 10 of U.S. report and sections 57 and 58 of the European report.

[g] Paragraph 15 of Part B of review of Article VI.

[h] Section 36 of the European report.

[i] Paragraph 4 of review of Articles I and II.

[j] Section 15 of U.S. report.

[k] Paragraph 4 of review of Articles I and II.

[l] Paragraph 5 of review of Articles I and II; paragraph 20 of review of Article IV; paragraph 14 of review of Article VII.

[m] Section 4 of U.S. report; sections 49–55 and 83 of European report.

[n] Paragraphs 11, 13 and 16 of review of Article III.

plutonium storage system,[o] its recognition of the importance of international and multilateral collaboration for arrangements regarding the back end of the fuel cycle,[p] and its noting of recommendations against *any* nuclear cooperation with Israel or South Africa,[q] the only relevant provisions of the Declaration are its commendation of the progress being made by the IAEA Committee on Assurances of Supply,[r] its criticism of unilateral modifications of supply agreements,[s] and its confirmation that:

> "each country's choices and decisions in the field of peaceful uses of nuclear energy should be respected without jeopardizing their respective fuel cycle policies. International co-operation in this area, including international transfer and subsequent operations should be governed by effective assurances of non-proliferation and predictable long-term supply assurances. The issuance of related licenses and authorizations involved should take place in a timely fashion."[t]

(The latter was adopted in lieu of a proposed paragraph that would have noted the particular sensitivity of facilities using or producing weapons-usable materials, and the desirability of due precautions in their export.)

7. The Declaration gives greater emphasis than either of the two panel reports to the relationship to non-proliferation of progress in nuclear arms control other than a comprehensive test ban treaty.[u]

8. The Declaration also gives greater emphasis than either of the panel reports to nuclear-weapon-free zones, including not only the Treaty of Tlatelolco, but efforts to achieve such zones in the Middle East and Africa, and the recently signed South Pacific Nuclear Weapons Free Zone Treaty.[v]

9. The Declaration includes a discussion of positive and negative security assurances,[w] which are also treated in the U.S. report.[x]

10. The Declaration also includes the observation that "the potential benefits of the peaceful applications of nuclear explosions have not been de-

---

[o] Paragraph 14 of review of Article III.
[p] Paragraph 19 of review of Article III and paragraph 9 of review of Article IV.
[q] See footnote l above.
[r] Paragraph 6 of review of Article IV.
[s] Paragraph 7 of review of Article IV.
[t] Paragraph 8 of review of Article IV.
[u] Compare review of Article VI with section 22 of U.S. report and page 41 and sections 1, 9, and 56–61 of the European report.
[v] Compare review of Article VII with Section 18 and the discussion of Israel, Argentina and Brazil in the U.S. report, and pages 42–43 above and sections 34, 92, and 93 of the European report.
[w] Paragraphs 15–20 of review of Article VII.
[x] Sections 11 and 12 of U.S. report.

monstrated"—which should help buttress one of the recommendations in the U.S. report.[y]

11. One topic dwelt upon in the Declaration that is not discussed in either of the panel reports is that of armed attacks on safeguarded nuclear facilities. Given impetus by the 1981 Israeli bombing of Iraq's research reactor and the subsequent Iraqi attacks on Iranian reactors, it states that any such attack should result in immediate action by the U.N. Security Council; encourages parties to be ready to provide immediate peaceful assistance to victims of such attacks; and urges cooperation in the efforts of the Geneva Disarmament Conference to evolve a multilateral treaty on the subject.[z]

12. There is no counterpart in the Declaration to the analyses of specific cases found in the two panel reports, or to their discussion of motivations, leverage, sanctions, bilateral approaches, or the potential role of particular countries or groups of countries. Likewise it contains nothing comparable to Parts II and III of the European report.

The adoption of this Declaration is encouraging and a significant milestone in international efforts to curb the further spread of nuclear weapons.

Final Declaration

Adopted by Consensus at the Third NPT Review Conference September 21, 1985

THE STATES PARTY TO THE TREATY ON THE NON-PROLIFERATION OF NUCLEAR WEAPONS WHICH MET IN GENEVA FROM 27 AUGUST TO 21 SEPTEMBER 1985 TO REVIEW THE OPERATION OF THE TREATY SOLEMNLY DECLARE:

—their conviction that the Treaty is essential to international peace and security,

—their continued support for the objectives of the Treaty which are:

    —the prevention of proliferation of nuclear weapons or other nuclear explosive devices;

    —the cessation of the nuclear arms race, nuclear disarmament and a Treaty on general and complete disarmament;

---

[y] Paragraph 3 of the Declaration's review of Article V. The recommendation is in Section 19(b) of the U.S. report, and referred to in its discussion of Pakistan, India, Argentina, and Brazil.

[z] Paragraphs 10–13 of review of Article IV.

—the promotion of co-operation between States Parties in the field of the peaceful uses of nuclear energy,

—the reaffirmation of their firm commitment to the purposes of the Preamble and the provisions of the Treaty,

—the determination to enhance the implementation of the Treaty and to further strengthen its authority.

Review of the Operation of the Treaty and Recommendations

Articles I and II and preambular paragraphs 1-3

The Conference noted the concerns and convictions expressed in preambular paragraphs 1 to 3 and agreed that they remain valid. The States Party to the Treaty remain resolved in their belief in the need to avoid the devastation that a nuclear war would bring. The Conference remains convinced that any proliferation of nuclear weapons would seriously increase the danger of a nuclear war.

The Conference agreed that the strict observance of the terms of Articles I and II remains central to achieving the shared objectives of preventing under any circumstances the further proliferation of nuclear weapons and preserving the Treaty's vital contribution to peace and security, including to the peace and security of non-Parties.

The Conference acknowledged the declarations by nuclear-weapons States Party to the Treaty that they had fulfilled their obligations under Article I. The Conference further acknowledged the declarations that non-nuclear-weapons States Party to the Treaty had fulfilled their obligations under Article II. The Conference was of the view therefore that one of the primary objectives of the Treaty had been achieved in the period under review.

The Conference also expressed deep concern that the national nuclear programmes of some States non-Party to the Treaty may lead them to obtain a nuclear weapon capability. States Party to the Treaty stated that any further detonation of a nuclear explosive device by any non-nuclear-weapon State would constitute a most serious breach of the non-proliferation objective.

The Conference noted the great and serious concerns expressed about the nuclear capability of South Africa and Israel. The Conference further noted the calls on all States for the total and complete prohibition of the transfer of all nuclear facilities, resources or devices to South Africa and Israel and to stop all exploitation of Namibian uranium, natural or enriched, until the attainment of Namibian independence.

Article III and preambular paragraphs 4 and 5

1. The Conference affirms its determination to strengthen further the barriers against the proliferation of nuclear weapons and other nuclear explosive devices to additional States. The spread of nuclear explosive capabilities would add immeasurably to regional and international tensions and suspicions. It would increase the risk of nuclear war and lessen the security of all States. The Parties remain convinced that universal adherence to the Non-Proliferation Treaty is the best way to strengthen the barriers against proliferation and they urge all States not party to the Treaty to accede to it. The Treaty and the régime of non-proliferation it supports play a central role in promoting regional and international peace and security, *inter alia*, by helping to prevent the spread of nuclear explosives. The non-proliferation and safeguards commitments in the Treaty are essential also for peaceful nuclear commerce and co-operation.

2. The Conference expresses the conviction that IAEA safeguards provide assurance that States are complying with their undertakings and assist States in demonstrating this compliance. They thereby promote further confidence among States and, being a fundamental element of the Treaty, help to strengthen their collective security. IAEA safeguards play a key role in preventing the proliferation of nuclear weapons and other nuclear explosive devices. Unsafeguarded nuclear activities in non-nuclear-weapon States pose serious proliferation dangers.

3. The Conference declares that the commitment to non-proliferation by nuclear-weapon States Party to the Treaty pursuant to Article I, by non-nuclear-weapon States Party to the Treaty pursuant to Article II, and by the acceptance of IAEA safeguards on all peaceful nuclear activities within non-nuclear-weapon States Party to the Treaty pursuant to Article III is a major contribution by those States to regional and international security. The Conference notes with satisfaction that the commitments in Articles I-III have been met and have greatly helped prevent the spread of nuclear explosives.

4. The Conference therefore specifically urges all non-nuclear-weapon States not party to the Treaty to make an international legally-binding commitment not to acquire nuclear weapons or other nuclear explosive devices and to accept IAEA safeguards on all their peaceful nuclear activities, both current and future, to verify that commitment. The Conference further urges all States in their international nuclear co-operation and in their nuclear export policies, and specifically as a necessary basis for the transfer of relevant nuclear supplies to non-nuclear-weapon States, to take effective steps towards achieving such a commitment to non-proliferation and acceptance of such safeguards by those States. The Conference expresses its view that ac-

cession to the Non-Proliferation Treaty is the best way to achieve that objective.

5. The Conference expresses its satisfaction that four of the five nuclear-weapon States have voluntarily concluded safeguards agreements with the IAEA, covering all or part of their peaceful nuclear activities. The Conference regards those agreements as further strengthening the non-proliferation régime and increasing the authority of IAEA and the effectiveness of its safeguards system. The Conference calls on the nuclear-weapon States to continue to co-operate fully with the IAEA in the implementation of these agreements and calls on IAEA to take full advantage of this co-operation. The Conference urges the People's Republic of China similarly to conclude a safeguards agreement with IAEA. The Conference recommends the continued pursuit of the principle of universal application of IAEA safeguards to all peaceful nuclear activities in all States. To this end, the Conference recognizes the value of voluntary offers and recommends further evaluation of the economic and practical possibility of extending application of safeguards to additional civil facilities in the nuclear-weapon States as and when IAEA resources permit and consideration of separation of the civil and military facilities in the nuclear-weapon States. Such an extending of safeguards will enable the further development and application of an effective régime in both nuclear-weapon States and non-nuclear-weapon States.

6. The Conference also affirms the great value to the non-proliferation régime of commitments by the nuclear-weapon States that nuclear supplies provided for peaceful use will not be used for nuclear weapons or other nuclear explosive purposes. Safeguards in nuclear-weapon States pursuant to their safeguards agreements with IAEA can verify observance of those commitments.

7. The Conference notes with satisfaction the adherence of further Parties to the Treaty and the conclusion of further safeguards agreements in compliance with the undertaking of the Treaty and recommends that:

   (a) The non-nuclear-weapon States Party to the Treaty that have not concluded the agreements required under Article III (4) conclude such agreements with IAEA as soon as possible;

   (b) The Director-General of IAEA intensify his initiative of submitting to States concerned draft agreements to facilitate the conclusion of corresponding safeguards agreements, and that Parties to the Treaty, in particular Depositary Parties, should actively support these initiatives;

   (c) All States Party to the Treaty make strenuous individual and collective efforts to make the Treaty truly universal.

8. The Conference notes with satisfaction that IAEA in carrying out its safeguards activities has not detected any diversion of a significant amount of safeguarded material to the production of nuclear weapons, other nuclear explosive devices or to purposes unknown.

9. The Conference notes that IAEA safeguards activities have not hampered the economic, scientific or technological development of the Parties to the Treaty, or international co-operation in peaceful nuclear activities and it urges that this situation be maintained.

10. The Conference commends IAEA on its implementation of safeguards pursuant to this Treaty and urges it to continue to ensure the maximum technical and cost effectiveness and efficiency of its operations, while maintaining consistency with the economic and safe conduct of nuclear activities.

11. The Conference notes with satisfaction the improvement of IAEA safeguards which has enabled it to continue to apply safeguards effectively during a period of rapid growth in the number of safeguarded facilities. It also notes that IAEA safeguards approaches are capable of adequately dealing with facilities under safeguards. In this regard, the recent conclusion of the project to design a safeguards régime for centrifuge enrichment plants and its implementation is welcomed. This project allows the application of an effective régime to all plants of this type in the territories both of nuclear-weapon States and non-nuclear-weapon States Parties to the Treaty.

12. The Conference emphasizes the importance of continued improvements in the effectiveness and efficiency of IAEA safeguards, for example, but not limited to:

    (a) Uniform and non-discriminatory implementation of safeguards;
    (b) The expeditious implementation of new instruments and techniques;
    (c) The further development of methods for evaluation of safeguards effectiveness in combination with safeguards information;
    (d) Continued increases in the efficiency of the use of human and financial resources and of equipment.

13. The Conference believes that further improvement of the list of materials and equipment which, in accordance with Article III (2) of the Treaty, calls for the application of IAEA safeguards should take account of advances in technology.

14. The Conference recommends that IAEA establish an internationally agreed effective system of international plutonium storage in accordance with Article XII(A)5 of its statute.

15. The Conference welcomes the significant contributions made by States Parties in facilitating the application of IAEA safeguards and in supporting research, development and other supports to further the application of effective and efficient safeguards. The Conference urges that such co-operation and support be continued and that other States Parties provide similar support.

16. The Conference calls upon all States to take IAEA safeguards requirements fully into account while planning, designing and constructing new nuclear fuel cycle facilities and while modifying existing nuclear fuel cycle facilities.

17. The Conference also calls on States Parties to the Treaty to assist IAEA in applying its safeguards, *inter alia,* through the efficient operation of State systems of accounting for and control of nuclear material, and including compliance with all notification requirements in accordance with safeguards agreements

18. The Conference welcomes the Agency's endeavours to recruit and train staff of the highest professional standards for safeguards implementation with due regard to the widest possible geographical distribution, in accordance with Article VII D of the IAEA Statute. It calls upon States to exercise their right regarding proposals of designation of IAEA inspectors in such a way as to facilitate the most effective use of safeguards manpower.

19. The Conference also commends to all States Parties the merits of establishment of international fuel cycle facilities, including multination participation, as a positive contribution to reassurance of the peaceful use and non-diversion of nuclear materials. While primarily a national responsibility, the Conference sees advantages in international co-operation concerning spent fuel storage and nuclear waste storage.

20. The Conference calls upon States Parties to continue their political, technical and financial support of the IAEA safeguards system.

21. The Conference underlines the need for IAEA to be provided with the necessary financial and human resources to ensure that the Agency is able to continue to meet effectively its safeguards responsibilities.

22. The Conference urges all States that have not done so to adhere to the Convention on the physical protection of nuclear material at the earliest possible date.

Article IV and prembular paragraphs 6 and 7

1. The Conference affirms that the NPT fosters the world-wide peaceful use of nuclear energy and reaffirms that nothing in the Treaty shall be interpreted as affecting the inalienable right of any Party to the Treaty to develop research, production and use of nuclear energy for peaceful purposes without discrimination and in conformity with Articles I and II.

2. The Conference reaffirms the undertaking by all Parties to the Treaty, in accordance with Article IV and preambular paragraphs 6 and 7, to facilitate the fullest possible exchange of equipment, materials and scientific and

technological information for the peaceful uses of nuclear energy and the right of all Parties to the Treaty to participate in such exchange. In this context, the Conference recognizes the importance of services. This can contribute to progress in general and to the elimination of technological and economic gaps between the developed and developing countries.

3. The Conference reaffirms the undertaking of the Parties to the Treaty in a position to do so to co-operate in contributing, alone or together with other States or international organizations, to the further development of the applications of nuclear energy for peaceful purposes, especially in the territories of the non-nuclear-weapon States Party to the Treaty, with due consideration for the needs of the developing areas of the world. In this context the Conference recognizes the particular needs of the least developed countries.

4. The Conference requests that States Parties consider possible bilateral co-operation measures to further improve the implementation of Article IV. To this end, States Parties are requested to give in written form their experiences in this area in the form of national contributions to be presented in a report to the next Review Conference.

5. The Conference recognizes the need for more predictable long-term supply assurances with effective assurances of non-proliferation.

6. The Conference commends the recent progress which the IAEA's Committee on Assurances of Supply (CAS) has made towards agreeing on a set of principles related to this matter, and expresses the hope that the Committee will complete this work soon. The Conference further notes with satisfaction the measures which CAS has recommended to the IAEA Board of Governors for alleviating technical and administrative problems in international shipments of nuclear items, emergency and back-up mechanisms, and mechanisms for the revision of international nuclear co-operation agreements and calls for the early completion of the work of CAS and the implementation of its recommendations.

7. The Conference reaffirms that in accordance with international law and applicable treaty obligations, States should fulfil their obligations under agreements in the nuclear field, and any modification of such agreements, if required, should be made only by mutual consent of the parties concerned.

8. The Conference confirms that each country's choices and decisions in the field of peaceful uses of nuclear energy should be respected without jeopardizing their respective fuel cycle policies. International co-operation in this area, including international transfer and subsequent operations should be governed by effective assurances of non-proliferation and predictable long-term supply assurances. The issuance of related licenses and authorization involved should take place in a timely fashion.

9. While recognizing that the operation and management of the back-end of the fuel cycle including nuclear waste storage are primarily a national responsibility, the Conference acknowledges the importance for the peaceful uses of nuclear energy of international and multilateral collaboration for arrangements in this area.

10. The Conference expresses its profound concern about the Israeli military attack on Iraq's safeguarded nuclear reactor on 7 June 1981. The Conference recalls Security Council Resolution 487 of 1981, strongly condemning the military attack by Israel which was unanimously adopted by the Council and which considered that the said attack constituted a serious threat to the entire IAEA safeguards régime which is the foundation of the Non-Proliferation Treaty. The Conference also takes note of the decisions and resolutions adopted by the United Nations General Assembly and the International Atomic Energy Agency on this attack, including Resolution 425 of 1984 adopted by the General Conference of the IAEA.

11. The Conference recognizes that an armed attack on a safeguarded nuclear facility, or threat of attack, would create a situation in which the Security Council would have to act immediately in accordance with provisions of the United Nations Charter. The Conference further emphasizes the responsibilities of the Depositaries of NPT in their capacity as permanent members of the Security Council to endeavour, in consultation with the other members of the Security Council, to give full consideration to all appropriate measures to be undertaken by the Security Council to deal with the situation, including measures under Chapter VII of the United Nations Charter.

12. The Conference encourages Parties to be ready to provide immediate peaceful assistance in accordance with international law to any Party to the NPT, if it so requests, whose safeguarded nuclear facilities have been subject to an armed attack, and calls upon all States to abide by any decisions taken by the Security Council in accordance with the United Nations Charter in relation to the attacking State.

13. The Conference considers that such attacks could involve grave dangers due to the release of radioactivity and that such attacks or threats of attack jeopardize the development of the peaceful uses of nuclear energy. The Conference also acknowledges that the matter is under consideration by the Conference on Disarmament and urges co-operation of all States for its speedy conclusion.

14. The Conference acknowledges the importance of the work of the International Atomic Energy Agency (IAEA) as the principal agent for technology transfer amongst the international organizations referred to in Article IV (2) and welcomes the successful operation of the Agency's technical assistance and co-operation programmes. The Conference records with appreciation that projects supported from these programmes covered a wide spectrum of

applications, related both to power and non-power uses of nuclear energy notably in agriculture, medicine, industry and hydrology. The Conference notes that the Agency's assistance to the developing States Party to the Treaty has been chiefly in the non-power uses of nuclear energy.

15. The Conference welcomes the establishment by the IAEA, following a recommendation of the First Review Conference of the Parties to the Treaty, of a mechanism to permit the channelling of extra-budgetary funds to projects additional to those financed from the IAEA Technical Assistance and Co-operation Fund. The Conference notes that this channel has been used to make additional resources available for a wide variety of projects in developing States Party to the Treaty.

16. In this context, the Conference proposes the following measures for consideration by the IAEA:

(i) IAEA assistance to developing countries in siting, construction, operation and safety of nuclear power projects and the associated trained manpower provision to be strengthened.

(ii) To provide, upon request, assistance in securing financing from outside sources for nuclear power projects in developing countries, and in particular the least developed countries.

(iii) IAEA assistance in nuclear planning systems for developing countries to be strengthened in order to help such countries draw up their own nuclear development plans.

(iv) IAEA assistance on country-specific nuclear development strategies to be further developed, with a view to identifying the application of nuclear technology that can be expected to contribute most to the development both of individual sectors and developing economies as a whole.

(v) Greater support for regional co-operative agreements, promoting regional projects based on regionally agreed priorities and using inputs from regional countries.

(vi) Exploration of the scope for multi-year, multi-donor projects financed from the extra-budgetary resources of the IAEA.

(vii) The IAEA's technical co-operation evaluation activity to be further developed, so as to enhance the Agency's effectiveness in providing technical assistance.

17. The Conference underlines the need for the provision to the IAEA of the necessary financial and human resources to ensure that the Agency is able to continue to meet effectively its responsibilities.

18. The Conference notes the appreciable level of bilateral co-operation in the peaceful uses of nuclear energy, and urges that States in a position to do so should continue and where possible increase the level of their co-operation in these fields.

19. The Conference urges that preferential treatment should be given to the non-nuclear-weapon States Party to the Treaty in access to or transfer of equipment, materials, services and scientific and technological information for the peaceful uses of nuclear energy, taking particularly into account needs of developing countries.

20. Great and serious concerns were expressed at the Conference about the nuclear capability of South Africa and Israel and that the development of such a capability by South Africa and Israel would undermine the credibility and stability of the non-proliferation Treaty régime. The Conference noted the demands made on all States to suspend any co-operation which would contribute to the nuclear programme of South Africa and Israel. The Conference further noted the demands made on South Africa and Israel to accede to the NPT, to accept IAEA safeguards on all their nuclear facilities and to pledge themselves not to manufacture or acquire nuclear weapons or other nuclear explosive devices.

21. The Conference recognizes the growing nuclear energy needs of the developing countries as well as the difficulties which the developing countries face in this regard, particularly with respect to financing their nuclear power programmes. The Conference calls upon States Party to the Treaty to promote the establishment of favourable conditions in national, regional and international financial institutions for financing of nuclear energy projects including nuclear power programmes in developing countries. Furthermore, the Conference calls upon the IAEA to initiate and the Parties to the Treaty to support the work of an expert group study on mechanisms to assist developing countries in the promotion of their nuclear power programmes, including the establishment of a Financial Assistance Fund.

22. The Conference recognizes that further IAEA assistance in the preparation of feasibility studies and infrastructure development might enhance the prospects for developing countries for obtaining finance, and recommends such countries as are members of the Agency to apply for such help under the Agency's technical assistance and co-operation programmes. The Conference also acknowledges that further support for the IAEA's Small and Medium Power Reactor (SMPR) Study could help the development of nuclear reactors more suited to the needs of some of the developing countries.

23. The Conference expresses its satisfaction at the progress in the preparations for the United Nations Conference for the Promotion of International Co-operation in the Peaceful Uses of Nuclear Energy (UNCPICPUNE) and its conviction that UNCPICPUNE will fully realize its goals in accordance with

the objectives of resolution 32/50 and relevant subsequent resolutions of the General Assembly for the development of national programmes of peaceful uses of nuclear energy for economic and social development, especially in the developing countries.

24. The Conference considers that all proposals related to the promotion and strengthening of international co-operation in the peaceful uses of nuclear energy which have been produced by the Third Review Conference of the NPT, be transmitted to the Preparatory Committee of the UNCPICPUNE.

Article V

1. The Conference reaffirms the obligation of Parties to the Treaty to take appropriate measures to ensure that potential benefits from any peaceful applications of nuclear explosions are made available to non-nuclear weapon States Party to the Treaty in full accordance with the provisions of Article V and other applicable international obligations, that such services should be provided to non-nuclear weapon States Party to the Treaty on a non-discriminatory basis and that the charge to such Parties for the explosive devices used should be as low as possible and exclude any charge for research and development.

2. The Conference confirms that the IAEA would be the appropriate international body through which any potential benefits of the peaceful applications of nuclear explosions could be made available to non-nuclear weapon States under the terms of Article V of the Treaty.

3. The Conference notes that the potential benefits of the peaceful applications of nuclear explosions have not been demonstrated and that no requests for services related to the peaceful applications of nuclear explosions have been received by the IAEA since the Second NPT Review Conference.

Article VI and preambular paragraphs 8–12

A.

1. The Conference recalled that under the provisions of Article VI all parties have undertaken to pursue negotiations in good faith:

—on effective measures relating to cessation of the nuclear arms race at an early date;

—on effective measures relating to nuclear disarmament;

—on a Treaty on general and complete disarmament under strict and effective international control.

2. The Conference undertook an evaluation of the achievements in respect of each aspect of the article in the period under review, and paragraphs 8 to 12 of the preamble, and in particular with regard to the goals set out in preambular paragraph 10 which recalls the determination expressed by the parties to the Partial Test Ban Treaty to:

> —continue negotiations to achieve the discontinuance of all test explosions of nuclear weapons for all time.

3. The Conference recalled the declared intention of the parties to the Treaty to achieve at the earliest possible date the cessation of the nuclear arms race and to undertake effective measures in the direction of nuclear disarmament and their urging made to all States parties to co-operate in the attainment of this objective. The Conference also recalled the determination expressed by the parties to the 1963 Treaty banning nuclear weapons tests in the atmosphere, in outer space and under water in its preamble to seek to achieve the discontinuance of all test explosions on nuclear weapons for all time and the desire to further the easing of international tension and the strengthening of trust between States in order to facilitate the cessation of the manufacture of nuclear weapons, the liquidation of all existing stockpiles, and the elimination from national arsenals of nuclear weapons and the means of their delivery.

4. The Conference notes that the Tenth Special Session of the General Assembly of the United Nations concluded, in paragraph 50 of its Final Document, that the achievement of nuclear disarmament will require urgent negotiations of agreements at appropriate stages and with adequate measures of verification satisfactory to the States concerned for:

(a) Cessation of the qualitative improvement and development of nuclear-weapon systems;

(b) Cessation of the production of all types of nuclear weapons and their means of delivery, and of the production of fissionable material for weapons purposes;

(c) A comprehensive, phased programme with agreed time-tables whenever feasible, for progressive and balanced reduction of stockpiles of nuclear weapons and their means of delivery, leading to their ultimate and complete elimination at the earliest possible time.

5. The Conference also recalled that in the Final Declaration of the First Review Conference, the parties expressed the view that the conclusion of a treaty banning all nuclear-weapon tests was one of the most important measures to halt the nuclear arms race and expressed the hope that the nuclear-weapon States Party to the Treaty would take the lead in reaching an early solution to the technical and political difficulties of this issue.

6. The Conference examined developments relating to the cessation of the nuclear arms race, in the period under review and noted in particular that the destructive potentials of the nuclear arsenals of nuclear-weapon States Parties, were undergoing continuing development, including a growing research and development component in military spending, continued nuclear testing, development of new delivery systems and their deployment.

7. The Conference noted the concerns expressed regarding developments with far reaching implications and the potential of a new environment, space, being drawn into the arms race. In that regard the Conference also noted the fact that the United States of America and the Union of Soviet Socialist Republics are pursuing bilateral negotiations on a broad complex of questions concerning space and nuclear arms, with a view to achieving effective agreements aimed at preventing an arms race in space and terminating it on Earth.

8. The Conference noted with regret that the development and deployment of nuclear weapon systems had continued during the period of review.

9. The Conference also took note of numerous proposals and actions, multilateral and unilateral, advanced during the period under review by many States with the aim of making progress towards the cessation of the nuclear arms race and nuclear disarmament.

10. The Conference examined the existing situation in the light of the undertaking assumed by the parties in Article VI to pursue negotiations in good faith on effective measures relating to cessation of the nuclear arms race at an early date and to nuclear disarmament. The Conference recalled that a stage of negotiations on the Strategic Arms Limitations Talks (SALT II) had been concluded in 1979, by the signing of the Treaty which had remained unratified. The Conference noted that both the Union of Soviet Socialist Republics and the United States of America have declared that they are abiding by the provisions of SALT II.

11. The Conference recalled that the bilateral negotiations between the Union of Soviet Socialist Republics and the United States of America which were held between 1981 and 1983 were discontinued without any concrete results.

12. The Conference noted that bilateral negotiations between the Union of Soviet Socialist Republics and the United States of America had been held in 1985 to consider questions concerning space and nuclear arms, both strategic and intermediate-range, with all the questions considered and resolved in their interrelationship. No agreement has emerged so far. These negotiations are continuing.

13. The Conference evaluated the progress made in multilateral nuclear disarmament negotiations in the period of the Review.

14. The Conference recalled that the trilateral negotiations on a comprehensive test ban treaty, begun in 1977 between the Union of Soviet Socialist Republics, the United Kingdom of Great Britain and Northern Ireland and the United States of America, had not continued after 1980, that the Committee on Disarmament and later the Conference on Disarmament had been called upon by the General Assembly of the United Nations in successive years to begin negotiations on such a Treaty, and noted that such negotiations had not been initiated, despite the submission of draft treaties and different proposals to the Conference on Disarmament in this regard.

15. The Conference noted the lack of progress on relevant items of the agenda of the Conference on Disarmament, in particular those relating to the cessation of the nuclear arms race and nuclear disarmament, the prevention of nuclear war including all related matters and effective international arrangements to assure non-nuclear-weapon States against the use or threat of use of nuclear weapons.

16. The Conference noted that two Review Conferences had taken place since 1980, one on the Sea-bed Treaty and one on the Environmental Modification Treaty and three General Conferences of the Agency for the Prohibition of Nuclear Weapons in Latin America. In 1982, a Special United Nations General Assembly Session on Disarmament took place without any results in matters directly linked to nuclear disarmament.

17. The Conference also noted the last five years had thus not given any results concerning negotiations on effective measures relating to cessation of the nuclear arms race and to nuclear disarmament.

B.

1. The Conference concluded that, since no agreements had been reached in the period under review on effective measures relating to the cessation of an arms race at an early date, on nuclear disarmament and on a Treaty on general and complete disarmament under strict and effective international control, the aspirations contained in preambular paragraphs 8 to 12 had still not been met, and the objectives under Article VI had not yet been achieved.

2. The Conference reiterated that the implementation of Article VI is essential to the maintenance and strengthening of the Treaty, reaffirmed the commitment of all States Parties to the implementation of this Article and called upon the States Parties to intensify their efforts to achieve fully the objectives of the Article. The Conference addressed a call to the nuclear-weapon States Parties in particular to demonstrate this commitment.

3. The Conference welcomes the fact that the United States of America and the Union of Soviet Socialist Republics are conducting bilateral negotiations on a complex of questions concerning space and nuclear arms—both strategic and intermediate-range—with all these questions considered and resolved

in their interrelationship. It hopes that these negotiations will lead to early and effective agreements aimed at preventing an arms race in space and terminating it on Earth, at limiting and reducing nuclear arms, and at strengthening strategic stability. Such agreements will complement and ensure the positive outcome of multilateral negotiations on disarmament, and would lead to the reduction of international tensions and the promotion of international peace and security. The Conference recalls that the two sides believe that ultimately the bilateral negotiations, just as efforts in general to limit and reduce arms, should lead to the complete elimination of nuclear arms everywhere.

4. The Conference urges the Conference on Disarmament, as appropriate, to proceed to early multilateral negotiations on nuclear disarmament in pursuance of paragraph 50 of the Final Document of the First Special Session of the General Assembly of the United Nations devoted to disarmament.

5. The Conference reaffirms the determination expressed in the preamble of the 1963 Partial Test Ban Treaty, confirmed in Article I (b) of the said Treaty and reiterated in preambular paragraph 10 of the Non-Proliferation Treaty, to achieve the discontinuance of all test explosions of nuclear weapons for all time.

6. The Conference also recalls that in the Final Document of the First Review Conference, the Parties expressed the view that the conclusion of a Treaty banning all nuclear weapons tests was one of the most important measures to halt the nuclear arms race. The Conference stresses the important contribution that such a treaty would make toward strengthening and extending the international barriers against the proliferation of nuclear weapons; it further stresses that adherence to such a treaty by all States would contribute substantially to the full achievement of the non-proliferation objective.

7. The Conference also took note of the appeals contained in five successive United Nations General Assembly resolutions since 1981 for a moratorium on nuclear weapons testing pending the conclusion of a Comprehensive Test Ban Treaty, and of similar calls made at this Conference. It also took note of the measure announced by the Union of Soviet Socialist Republics for a unilateral moratorium on all nuclear explosions from 6 August 1985 until 1 January 1986, which would continue beyond that date if the United States of America, for its part, refrained from carrying out nuclear explosions. The Union of Soviet Socialist Republics suggested that this would provide an example for other nuclear-weapon States and would create favourable conditions for the conclusion of a Comprehensive Test Ban Treaty and the promotion of the fuller implementation of the Non-Proliferation Treaty.

8. The Conference took note of the unconditional invitation extended by the United States of America to the Union of Soviet Socialist Republics to send

observers, who may bring any equipment they deem necessary, to measure a United States of America nuclear test in order to begin a process which in the view of the United States of America would help to ensure effective verification of limitations on under-ground nuclear testing.

9. The Conference also took note of the appeals contained in five United Nations General Assembly resolutions since 1982 for a freeze on all nuclear weapons in quantitative and qualitative terms, which should be taken by all nuclear-weapon States or, in the first instance and simultaneously, by the Union of Soviet Socialist Republics and the United States of America on the understanding that the other nuclear-weapon States would follow their example, and of similar calls made at this Conference.

10. The Conference took note of proposals by the Union of Soviet Socialist Republics and the United States of America for the reduction of nuclear weapons.

11. The Conference took note of proposals submitted by States Parties on a number of related issues relevant to achieving the purposes of Article VI and set out in Annex I to this document and in the statements made in the General Debate of the Conference.

12. The Conference reiterated its conviction that the objectives of Article VI remained unfulfilled and concluded that the nuclear-weapon States should make greater efforts to ensure effective measures for the cessation of the nuclear arms race at an early date, for nuclear disarmament and for a Treaty on general and complete disarmament under strict and effective international control.

[13.] The Conference expressed the hope for rapid progress in the United States-USSR bilateral negotiations.

[14.] The Conference except for certain States whose views are reflected in the following subparagraph deeply regretted that a comprehensive multilateral Nuclear Test Ban Treaty banning all nuclear tests by all States in all environments for all time had not been concluded so far and, therefore, called on the nuclear-weapon States Party to the Treaty to resume trilateral negotiations in 1985 and called on all the nuclear-weapon States to participate in the urgent negotiation and conclusion of such a Treaty as a matter of the highest priority in the Conference on Disarmament.

[15.] At the same time, the Conference noted that certain States Party to the Treaty, while committed to the goal of an effectively verifiable comprehensive Nuclear Test Ban Treaty, considered deep and verifiable reductions in existing arsenals of nuclear weapons as the highest priority in the process of pursuing the objectives of Article VI.

[16.] The Conference also noted the statement of the USSR, as one of the nuclear weapon States Party to the Treaty, recalling its repeatedly expressed readiness to proceed forthwith to negotiations, trilateral and multilateral, with the aim of concluding a comprehensive Nuclear Test Ban Treaty and the submission by it of a draft Treaty proposal to this end.

Article VII and the Security of Non-Nuclear-Weapon States

1. The Conference observes the growing interest in utilizing the provisions of Article VII of the Non-Proliferation Treaty, which recognizes the right of any group of States to conclude regional treaties in order to assure the absence of nuclear weapons in their respective territories.

2. The Conference considers that the establishment of nuclear-weapon-free zones on the basis of arrangements freely arrived at among the States of the region concerned constitutes an important disarmament measure and therefore the process of establishing such zones in different parts of the world should be encouraged with the ultimate objective of achieving a world entirely free of nuclear weapons. In the process of establishing such zones, the characteristics of each region should be taken into account.

3. The Conference emphasizes the importance of concluding nuclear-weapon-free zone arrangements in harmony with internationally recognized principles, as stated in the Final Document of the First Special Session of the United Nations devoted to disarmament.

4. The Conference holds the view that, under appropriate conditions, progress towards the establishment of nuclear-weapon-free zones will create conditions more conducive to the establishment of zones of peace in certain regions of the world.

5. The Conference expresses its belief that concrete measures of nuclear disarmament would significantly contribute to creating favourable conditions for the establishment of nuclear-weapon-free zones.

6. The Conference expresses its satisfaction at the continued successful operation of the Treaty for the Prohibition of Nuclear Weapons in Latin America (Treaty of Tlatelolco). It reaffirms the repeated exhortations of the General Assembly to France, which is already a signatory of Additional Protocol I, to ratify it, and calls upon the Latin American States that are eligible to become parties to the treaty to do so. The Conference welcomes the signature and ratification of Additional Protocol II to this Treaty by all nuclear-weapon States.

7. The Conference also notes the continued existence of the Antarctic Treaty.

8. The Conference notes the endorsement of the South Pacific Nuclear Free Zone Treaty by the South Pacific Forum on 6 August 1985 at Rarotonga and

welcomes this achievement as consistent with Article VII of the Non-Proliferation Treaty. The Conference also takes note of the draft Protocols to the South Pacific Nuclear Free Zone Treaty and further notes the agreement at the South Pacific Forum that consultations on the Protocols should be held between members of the Forum and the nuclear-weapon States eligible to sign them.

9. The Conference takes note of the existing proposals and the ongoing regional efforts to achieve nuclear-weapon-free zones in different areas of the world.

10. The Conference recognizes that for the maximum effectiveness of any treaty arrangements for establishing a nuclear-weapon-free zone the co-operation of the nuclear-weapon States is necessary. In this connection, the nuclear-weapon States are invited to assist the efforts of States to create nuclear-weapon-free zones, and to enter into binding undertakings to respect strictly the status of such a zone and to refrain from the use or threat of use of nuclear weapons against the States of the zone.

11. The Conference welcomes the consensus reached by the United Nations General Assembly at its thirty-fifth session that the establishment of a nuclear-weapon-free zone in the region of the Middle East would greatly enhance international peace and security, and urges all parties directly concerned to consider seriously taking the practical and urgent steps required for the implementation of the proposal to establish a nuclear-weapon-free zone in the region of the Middle East.

12. The Conference also invites the nuclear-weapon States and all other States to render their assistance in the establishment of the zone and at the same time to refrain from any action that runs counter to the letter and spirit of United Nations General Assembly resolution 39/54.

13. The Conference considers that acceding to the Non-Proliferation Treaty and acceptance of IAEA safeguards by all States in the region of the Middle East will greatly facilitate the creation of a nuclear-weapon-free zone in the region and will enhance the credibility of the Treaty.

14. The Conference considers that the development of a nuclear-weapon capability by South Africa at any time frustrates the implementation of the Declaration on the Denuclearization of Africa and that collaboration with South Africa in this area would undermine the credibility and the stability of the Non-Proliferation Treaty régime. South Africa is called upon to submit all its nuclear installations and facilities to IAEA safeguards and to accede to the Non-Proliferation Treaty. All States Parties directly concerned are urged to consider seriously taking the practical and urgent steps required for the implementation of the proposal to establish a nuclear-weapon-free zone in Africa. The nuclear-weapon States are invited to assist the efforts of States to create a nuclear-weapon-free zone in Africa, and to enter into binding un-

dertakings to respect strictly the status of such a zone and to refrain from the use or threat of use of nuclear weapons against the States of the zone.

15. The Conference considers that the most effective guarantee against the possible use of nuclear weapons and the danger of nuclear war is nuclear disarmament and the complete elimination of nuclear weapons. Pending the achievement of this goal on a universal basis and recognizing the need for all States to ensure their independence, territorial integrity and sovereignty, the Conference reaffirms the particular importance of assuring and strengthening the security of non-nuclear-weapon States Parties which have renounced the acquisition of nuclear weapons. The Conference recognizes that different approaches may be required to strengthen the security of non-nuclear-weapon States Parties to the Treaty.

16. The Conference underlines again the importance of adherence to the Treaty by non-nuclear-weapon States as the best means of reassuring one another of their renunciation of nuclear weapons and as one of the effective means of strengthening their mutual security.

17. The Conference takes note of the continued determination of the Depositary States to honour their statements, which were welcomed by the United Nations Security Council in resolution 255 (1968), that, to ensure the security of the non-nuclear-weapon States Parties to the Treaty, they will provide or support immediate assistance, in accordance with the Charter, to any non-nuclear-weapon State Party to the Treaty which is a victim of an act or an object of a threat of aggression in which nuclear weapons are used.

18. The Conference reiterates its conviction that, in the interest of promoting the objectives of the Treaty, including the strengthening of the security of non-nuclear-weapon States Parties, all States, both nuclear-weapon and non-nuclear-weapon States, should refrain, in accordance with the Charter of the United Nations, from the threat or the use of force in relations between States, involving either nuclear or non-nuclear weapons.

19. The Conference recalls that the Tenth Special Session of the General Assembly in paragraph 59 of the Final Document took note of the declarations made by the nuclear-weapon States regarding the assurance of non-nuclear-weapon States against the use or threat of use of nuclear weapons and urged them to pursue efforts to conclude, as appropriate, effective arrangements to assure non-nuclear-weapon States against the use or threat of use of nuclear weapons.

20. Being aware of the consultations and negotiations on effective international arrangements to assure non-nuclear-weapon States against the use or threat of use of nuclear weapons, which have been under way in the Conference on Disarmament for several years, the Conference regrets that the search for a common approach which could be included in an international legally binding instrument, has been unsuccessful. The Conference takes

note of the repeatedly expressed intention of the Conference on Disarmament to continue to explore ways and means to overcome the difficulties encountered in its work and to carry out negotiations on the question of effective international arrangements to assure non-nuclear-weapon States against the use or threat of use of nuclear weapons. In this connection, the Conference calls upon all States, particularly the nuclear-weapon States, to continue the negotiations in the Conference on Disarmament devoted to the search for a common approach acceptable to all, which could be included in an international instrument of a legally binding character.

Article VIII

The States Party to the Treaty participating in the Conference propose to the Depositary Governments that a fourth Conference to review the operation of the Treaty be convened in 1990.

The Conference accordingly invites States Party to the Treaty which are Members of the United Nations to request the Secretary-General of the United Nations to include the following item in the provisional agenda of the forty-third session of the General Assembly:

"Implementation of the conclusions of the third Review Conference of the Parties to the Treaty on the Non-Proliferation of Nuclear Weapons and establishment of a Preparatory Committee for the fourth Conference."

Article IX

The Conference, having expressed great satisfaction that the overwhelming majority of States have acceded to the Treaty on the Non-Proliferation of Nuclear Weapons and having recognized the urgent need for further ensuring the universality of the Treaty, appeals to all States, particularly the nuclear-weapon States and other States advanced in nuclear technology, which have not yet done so, to adhere to the Treaty at the earliest possible date.

Appendix D: Nuclear Suppliers' Group Guidelines for Nuclear Transfers

1. The following fundamental principles for safeguards and export controls should apply to nuclear transfers to any non-nuclear-weapon state for peaceful purposes. In this connection, suppliers have defined an export trigger list and agreed on common criteria for technology transfers.

Prohibition on nuclear explosives

2. Suppliers should authorise transfer of items identified in the trigger list only upon formal government assurances from recipients explicitly excluding uses which would result in any nuclear explosive device.

Physical protection

3. (a) All nuclear materials and facilities identified by the agreed trigger list should be placed under effective physical protection to prevent unauthorised use and handling. The levels of physical protection to be ensured in relation to the type of materials, equipment and facilities, have been agreed by suppliers, taking account of international recommendations.

(b) The implementation of measures of physical protection in the recipient country is the responsibility of the government of that country. However, in order to implement the terms agreed upon amongst suppliers, the levels of physical protection on which these measures have to be based should be the subject of an agreement between supplier and recipient.

(c) In each case special arrangements should be made for a clear definition of responsibilities for the transport of trigger list items.

Safeguards

4. Suppliers should transfer trigger list items only when covered by IAEA safeguards, with duration and coverage provisions in conformance with the GOV/1621 guidelines. Exceptions should be made only after consultation with the parties to this understand.

5. Suppliers will jointly reconsider their common safeguards requirements, whenever appropriate.

Safeguards triggered by the transfer of certain technology

6. (a) The requirements of paragraphs 2, 3 and 4 above should also apply to facilities for reprocessing, enrichment, or heavy water production, utilising technology directly transferred by the supplier or derived from transferred facilities, or major critical components thereof.

(b) The transfer of such facilities, or major critical components thereof, or related technology, should require an undertaking (1) that IAEA safeguards apply to any facilities of the same type (i.e. if the design, construction or operating processes are based on the same or similar physical or chemical processes, as defined in the trigger list) constructed during an agreed period in the recipient country and (2) that there should at all times be in effect safeguards agreement permitting the IAEA to apply Agency safeguards with respect to such facilities identified by the recipient, or by the supplier in consultation with the recipient, as using transferred technology.

Special controls on sensitive exports

7. Suppliers should exercise restraint in the transfer of sensitive facilities, technology and weapons-usable materials. If enrichment or reprocessing facilities, equipment or technology are to be transferred, suppliers should encourage recipients to accept, as an alternative to national plants, supplier involvement and/or other appropriate multi-national participation in resulting facilities. Suppliers should also promote international (including IAEA) activities concerned with multi-national regional fuel cycle centres.

Special controls on export of enrichment facilities, equipment and technology

8. For a transfer of an enrichment facility, or technology therefor, the recipient nation should agree that neither the transferred facility, nor any facility based on such technology, will be designed or operated for the production of greater than 20% enriched uranium without the consent of the supplier nation, of which the IAEA should be advised.

Controls on supplied or derived weapons-usable material

9. Suppliers recognise the importance, in order to advance the objectives of these guidelines and to provide opportunities further to reduce the risks of proliferation, of including in agreements on supply of nuclear materials or of facilities which produce weapons-usable material, provisions calling for mutual agreement between the supplier and the recipient on arrangements for re-processing, storage, alteration, use, transfer or retransfer of any weapons-usable material involved. Suppliers should endeavour to include such provisions whenever appropriate and practicable.

Controls on retransfer

10. (a) Suppliers should transfer trigger list items, including technology defined under paragraph 6, only upon the recipient's assurance that in the case of:

(1) transfer of such items,
or
(2) transfer of trigger list items derived from facilities originally transferred by the supplier, or with the help of equipment or technology originally transferred by the supplier;

the recipient of the retransfer or transfer will have provided the same assurances as those required by the supplier for the original transfer.

(b) In addition the supplier's consent should be required for:

(1) any retransfer of the facilities major critical components, or technology described in paragraph 6;

(2) any transfer of facilities or major critical components derived from those items:

(3) any retransfer of heavy water or weapons-usable material.

Physical security

11. Suppliers should promote international co-operation on the exchange of physical security information, protection of nuclear materials in transit, and recovery of stolen nuclear materials and equipment.

Support for effective IAEA safeguards

12. Suppliers should make special efforts in support of effective implementation of IAEA safeguards. Suppliers should also support the Agency's efforts to assist member states in the improvement of their national systems of accounting and control of nuclear material and to increase the technical effectiveness of safeguards.

Similarly, they should make every effort to support the IAEA in increasing further the adequacy of safeguards in the light of technical developments and the rapidly growing number of nuclear facilities, and to support appropriate initiatives aimed at improving the effectiveness of IAEA safeguards.

Sensitive plant design features

13. Suppliers should encourage the designers and makers of sensitive equipment to construct it in such a way as to facilitate the application of safeguards.

Consultations

14. (a) Suppliers should maintain contact and consult through regular channels on matters connected with the implementation of these guidelines.

(b) Suppliers should consult, as each deems appropriate, with other Governments concerned on specific sensitive cases, to ensure that any transfer does not contribute to risks of conflict or instability.

(c) In the event that one or more suppliers believe that there has been a violation of supplier/recipient understandings resulting from these guidelines, particularly in the case of an explosion of a nuclear device, or illegal termination or violation of IAEA safeguards by a recipient, suppliers should consult promptly through diplomatic channels in order to determine and assess the reality and extent of the alleged violation.

Pending the early outcome of such consultations, suppliers will not act in a manner that could prejudice any measure that may be adopted by other suppliers concerning their current contacts with that recipient.

Upon the findings of such consultations, the suppliers, bearing in mind Article XII of the IAEA Statute, should agree on an appropriate response and possible action which could include the termination of nuclear transfers to that recipient.

15. In considering transfers, each supplier should exercise prudence having regard to all the circumstances of each case, including any risk that technology transfers not covered by paragraph 6, or subsequent retransfers, might result in unsafeguarded nuclear materials.

16. Unanimous consent is required for any changes in these guidelines, including any which might result from the reconsideration mentioned in paragraph 5.

21 September 1977

Countries applying the London Guidelines as of May 1985

I. Countries which participated in the 1975-77 negotiations:

Canada	Union of Soviet Socialist Republics
Federal Republic of Germany	United Kingdom
France	United States
Japan	

II. Countries which joined Group I in applying the Guidelines by 11th January 1978:

Belgium	The Netherlands
Czechoslovakia	Poland
German Democratic Republic	Sweden
Italy	Switzerland

III. Countries which informed the IAEA afterwards by letter that they would apply the Guidelines:

Australia (Feb. 1978)	Luxembourg (Nov. 1984)
Finland (Jan. 1980)	Ireland (Nov. 1984)
Denmark (Aug. 1984)	Bulgaria (Dec. 1984)
Greece (Aug. 1984)	

IV. South Africa

South Africa announced in 1984 that it would follow the Guidelines in its export policy.

Appendix E: Declaration of common policy on the consequences of the adoption of the London Guidelines by the ten member states of the Community

20 November 1984

The Ten, meeting within the framework of European political cooperation (hereafter referred to as the "Member States"):

— Mindful of the rights and obligations arising from the membership of
the Member States of the European Atomic Energy Community;

— Recording their support for the objective of the non-proliferation of
nuclear weapons;

— Referring to the various undertakings regarding the peaceful use of
nuclear energy and control which the Member States have made
respectively, especially the Treaty on the Non-Proliferation of
Nuclear Weapons and the agreements concluded between the
Member States, the European Atomic Energy Community and the
International Atomic Energy Agency for the application of safeguards
within the Community;

— Noting the adoption by all the Member States of the Guidelines for
the Export of Nuclear Material, Equipment and Technology, in the
capacity of unilateral undertakings as published in circular INFCIRC/
254 of the International Atomic Energy Agency (hereinafter referred
to as the "Guidelines").

1. Take note that the principles of the Guidelines form a basic common
discipline for the Member States for their nuclear exports;

2. Take note that, with due regard for the Treaties of Rome and within
the framework of the competence of the Member States, transfers of
nuclear materials, equipment or technology may take place without
restriction between the Member States, subject to the following
additional detailed rules:

   2.1 Until they are used, separated plutonium and greater than 20%
enriched uranium shall be stored by the Member States at the
place where it has been separated or enriched to more than
20% *or* at the place of manufacture of fuel containing
plutonium or greater than 20% enriched uranium *or* at a storage
place set up and administered by a Member State *or* at a place
decided on by joint agreement by the Member States
concerned.

   2.1.1 Plutonium and greater than 20% enriched uranium shall be
transferred by the Member States on submission of a consignee certificate (Model form in Annex) specifying the ultimate

destination, the quantity, the approximate delivery timetable, the use timetable, the form in which delivery will take place and the use of such material for one or other of the following purposes:

— fuelling any functioning power reactor or research reactor or one that is in the course of construction on the territory of a Member State or under its jurisdiction;

— processing on the territory of a Member State or under its jurisdiction for fuelling the above mentioned reactors or, subject to the detailed rules laid down in paragraph 2.1.3, for fuelling any reactor situated on the territory of a third State;

— research and development in any laboratory situated on the territory of a Member State or under its jurisdiction. Subject to the detailed rules of paragraph 2.1.3, the material may also be transferred to a third State under the framework of co-operation in the field of research and development;

— use in any other facility relating to an energy programme or one of research and development and situated on the territory of a Member State or under its jurisdiction;

including the intermediate storage required for the smooth functioning of the above mentioned operations.

2.1.2 The Government of the Member States to which the consignee belongs shall certify the information given in the certificate referred to in paragraph 2.1.1.

2.1.3 Plutonium and greater than 20% enriched uranium shall not be re-transferred to a third State without the mutual agreement of the Member State which separated it or enriched it to more than 20% and of the Member State wishing to effect a re-transfer, without prejudice to any other rights of prior consent which might exist.

2.1.4 Paragraphs 2.1.1, 2.1.2 and 2.1.3 above shall not apply to:
— plutonium with an isotopic value in plutonium 238 greater than 80%;
— special fissile products used in quantities of one gramme or less as a sensitive component of measuring instruments;
— transfers which do not exceed 50 grammes in effect made in the course of one year to a given Member State;
— retransfers which do not exceed 50 grammes in the course of one year to a given third State, without prejudice to any other rights of prior consent which might exist.

2.1.5 The foregoing detailed rules shall be reviewed by the Member States should a system of international plutonium storage be set up under the auspices of the International Atomic Energy Agency.

2.2   Facilities and technology for reprocessing, enrichment and heavy-water production or facilities set up on the basis of the said technology may be transferred taking into account the nature and development of the nuclear programmes of the consignee Member States.

2.3   No enriching facility transferred from a Member State, nor any facility set up on the basis of the technology of such a facility shall be designed or operated for the production of greater than 20% enriched uranium without the agreement of the supplier Member States.

2.4   When sensitive facilities or technology are being transferred, the Member States will observe the provisions relating to protection of confidentiality.

2.5   The prior agreement of the supplier State shall be required for any retransfer of facilities, major critical components for reprocessing, enriching or heavy-water production and for any transfer of facilities or major critical components derived from the said articles.

The said retransfers and transfers between Member States may take place after consultation with the Member State of origin taking into account the nature and development of the nuclear programme of the consignee Member State.

3. Take note that the Member States shall apply to the nuclear material under their jurisdiction measures of physical protection that are at least equal to the levels fixed by the Guidelines.

4. Take note that, under the above mentioned conditions, transfers between Member States of nuclear material, equipment or technology shall take place in a manner compatible with the requirements of non-proliferation and of free movement.

Appendix F: Convention on the Physical Protection of Nuclear Material

Signed at New York March 3, 1980
Ratification advised by U.S. Senate July 30, 1981
Ratified by U.S. President September 4, 1981

The States Parties to This Convention,

Recognizing the right of all States to develop and apply nuclear energy for peaceful purposes and their legitimate interests in the potential benefits to be derived from the peaceful application of nuclear energy,

Convinced of the need for facilitating international co-operation in the peaceful application of nuclear energy,

Desiring to avert the potential dangers posed by the unlawful taking and use of nuclear material,

Convinced that offenses relating to nuclear material are a matter of grave concern and that there is an urgent need to adopt appropriate and effective measures to ensure the prevention, detection and punishment of such offenses,

Aware of the Need for international co-operation to establish, in conformity with the national law of each State Party and with this Convention, effective measures for the physical protection of nuclear material,

Convinced that this Convention should facilitate the safe transfer of nuclear material,

Stressing also the importance of the physical protection of nuclear material in domestic use, storage and transport,

Recognizing the importance of effective physical protection of nuclear material used for military purposes, and understanding that such material is and will continue to be accorded stringent physical protection,

Have Agreed as follows:

Article 1

For the purposes of this Convention:

(a) "nuclear material" means plutonium except that with istotopic concentration exceeding 80% in plutonium-238; uranium-233; uranium enriched in the isotopes 235 or 233; uranium containing the mixture of isotopes as occurring in nature other than in the form of ore or ore-residue; any material containing one or more of the foregoing;

(b) "uranium enriched in the 235 or 233" means uranium containing the isotopes 235 or 233 or both in an amount such that the abundance ratio of the sum of these isotopes to the isotope 238 is greater than the ratio of the isotope 235 to the isotope 238 occurring in nature;

(c) "international nuclear transport" means the carriage of a consignment of nuclear material by any means of transportation intended to go beyond the territory of the State where the shipment originates beginning with the departure from a facility of the shipper in that State and ending with the arrival at a facility of the receiver within the State of ultimate destination.

Article 2

1. The Convention shall apply to nuclear material used for peaceful purposes while in international nuclear transport.

2. With the exception of articles 3 and 4 and paragraph 3 of article 5, this Convention shall also apply to nuclear material used for peaceful purposes while in domestic use, storage and transport.

3. Apart from the commitments expressly undertaken by States Parties in the articles covered by paragraph 2 with respect to nuclear material used for peaceful purposes while in domestic use, storage and transport, nothing in this Convention shall be interpreted as affecting the sovereign rights of a State regarding the domestic use, storage and transport of such nuclear material.

Article 3

Each State Party shall take appropriate steps within the framework of its national law and consistent with international law to ensure as far as practicable that, during international nuclear transport, nuclear material within its territory, or on board a ship or aircraft under its jurisdiction insofar as such ship or aircraft is engaged in the transport to or from that State, is protected at the levels described in Annex I.

Article 4

1. Each State Party shall not export or authorize the export of nuclear material

unless the State Party has received assurances that such material will be protected during the international nuclear transport at the levels described in Annex I.

2. Each State Party shall not import or authorize the import of nuclear material from a State not party to this Convention unless the State Party has received assurances that such material will during the international nuclear transport be protected at the levels described in Annex I.

3. A State Party shall not allow the transit of its territory by land or internal waterways or through its airports or seaports of nuclear material between States that are not parties to this Convention unless the State Party has received assurances as far as practicable that this nuclear material will be protected during international nuclear transport at the levels described in Annex I.

4. Each State Party shall apply within the framework of its national law the levels of physical protection described in Annex I to nuclear material being transported from a part of that State to another part of the same State through international waters or airspace.

5. The State Party responsible for receiving assurances that the nuclear material will be protected at the levels described in Annex I according to paragraphs 1 to 3 shall identify and inform in advance States which the nuclear material is expected to transit by land or internal waterways, or whose airports or seaports it is expected to enter.

6. The responsibility for obtaining assurances referred to in paragraph 1 may be transferred, by mutual agreement, to the State Party involved in the transport as the importing State.

7. Nothing in this article shall be interpreted as in any way affecting the territorial sovereignty and jurisdiction of a State, including that over its airspace and territorial sea.

Article 5

1. States Parties shall identify and make known to each other directly or through the International Atomic Energy Agency their central authority and point of contact having responsibility for physical protection of nuclear material and for co-ordinating recovery and response operations in the event of any unauthorized removal, use or alteration of nuclear material or in the event of credible threat thereof.

2. In the case of theft, robbery or any other unlawful taking of nuclear material or of credible threat thereof, States Parties shall, in accordance with their national law, provide co-operation and assistance to the maximum feasible ex-

tent in the recovery and protection of such material to any State that so requests. In particular:

(a) a State Party shall take appropriate steps to inform as soon as possible other States, which appear to it to be concerned, of any theft, robbery or other unlawful taking of nuclear material or credible threat thereof and to inform, where appropriate, international organizations;

(b) as appropriate, the States Parties concerned shall exchange information with each other or international organizations with a view to protecting threatened nuclear material, verifying the integrity of the shipping container, or recovering unlawfully taken nuclear material and shall:

(i) co-ordinate their efforts through diplomatic and other agreed channels;

(ii) render assistance, if requested;

(iii) ensure the return of nuclear material stolen or missing as a consequence of the above-mentioned events.

The means of implementation of this co-operation shall be determined by the States Parties concerned.

3. States Parties shall co-operate and consult as appropriate, with each other directly or through international organizations, with a view to obtaining guidance on the design, maintenance and improvement of systems of physical protection of nuclear material in international transport.

Article 6

1. States Parties shall take appropriate measures consistent with their national law to protect the confidentiality of any information which they receive in confidence by virtue of the provisions of this Convention from another State Party or through participation in an activity carried out for the implementation of this Convention. If States Parties provide information to international organizations in confidence, steps shall be taken to ensure that the confidentiality of such information is protected.

2. States Parties shall not be required by this Convention to provide any information which they are not permitted to communicate pursuant to national law or which would jeopardize the security of the State concerned or the physical protection of nuclear material.

Article 7

1. The intentional commission of:

(a) an act without lawful authority which constitutes the receipt, possession, use, transfer, alteration, disposal or dispersal of nuclear material and which causes or is likely to cause death or serious injury to any person or substantial damage to property;

(b) a theft or robbery of nuclear material;

(c) an embezzlement or fraudulent obtaining of nuclear material;

(d) an act constituting a demand for nuclear material by threat or use of force or by any other form of intimidation;

(e) a threat:

(i) to use nuclear material to cause death or serious injury to any person or substantial property damage, or

(ii) to commit an offense described in subparagraph (b) in order to compel a natural or legal person, international organization or State to do or to refrain from doing any act:

(f) an attempt to commit any offense described in paragraphs (a), (b) or (c); and

(g) an act which constitutes participation in any offense described in paragraphs (a) to (f) shall be made a punishable offense by each State Party under its national law.

2. Each State Party shall make the offenses described in this article punishable by appropriate penalties which take into account their grave nature.

Article 8

1. Each State Party shall take such measures as may be necessary to establish its jurisdiction over the offenses set forth in article 7 in the following cases:

(a) when the offense is committed in the territory of that State or on board a ship or aircraft registered in that State;

(b) when the alleged offender is a national of that State.

2. Each State Party shall likewise take such measures as may be necessary to establish its jurisdiction over these offenses in cases where the alleged offender is present in its territory and it does not extradite him pursuant to article 11 to any of the States mentioned in paragraph 1.

3. This Convention does not exclude any criminal jurisdiction exercised in accordance with national law.

4. In addition to the State Parties mentioned in paragraphs 1 and 2, each State Party may, consistent with international law, establish its jurisdiction over the offenses set forth in article 7 when it is involved in international nuclear transport as the exporting or importing State.

Article 9

Upon being satisfied that the circumstances so warrant, the State Party in whose territory the alleged offender is present shall take appropriate measures, including detention, under its national law to ensure his presence for the purpose of prosecution or extradition. Measures taken according to this article shall be notified without delay to the States required to establish jurisdiction pursuant to article 8 and, where appropriate, all other States concerned.

Article 10

The State Party in whose territory the alleged offender is present shall, if it does not extradite him, submit, without exception whatsoever and without undue delay, the case to its competent authorities for the purpose of prosecution, through proceedings in accordance with the laws of that State.

Article 11

1. The offenses in article 7 shall be deemed to be included as extraditable offenses in any extradition treaty existing between States Parties. States Parties undertake to include those offenses as extraditable offenses in every future extradition treaty to be concluded between them.

2. If a State Party which makes extradition conditional on the existence of a treaty receives a request for extradition from another State Party with which it has no extradition treaty, it may at its option consider this Convention as the legal basis for extradition in respect of those offenses. Extradition shall be subject to the other conditions provided by the law of the requested State.

3. States Parties which do not make extradition conditional on the existence of a treaty shall recognize those offenses as extraditable offenses between themselves subject to the conditions provided by the law of the requested State.

4. Each of the offenses shall be treated, for the purpose of extradition between States Parties, as if it had been committed not only in the place in which it occurred but also in the territories of the States Parties required to establish their jurisdiction in accordance with paragraph 1 of article 8.

Article 12

Any person regarding whom proceedings are being carried out in connection with any of the offenses set forth in article 7 shall be guaranteed fair treatment at all stages of the proceedings.

Article 13

1. States Parties shall afford one another the greatest measure of assistance in connection with criminal proceedings brought in respect of the offenses set forth in article 7, including the supply of evidence at their disposal necessary for the proceedings. The law of the State requested shall apply in all cases.

2. The provisions of paragraph 1 shall not affect obligations under any other treaty, bilateral or multilateral, which governs or will govern, in whole or in part, mutual assistance in criminal matters.

Article 14

1. Each State Party shall inform the depositary of its laws and regulations which give effect to this Convention. The depositary shall communicate such information periodically to all States Parties.

2. The State Party where an alleged offender is prosecuted shall, wherever practicable, first communicate the final outcome of the proceedings to the States directly concerned. The State Party shall also communicate the final outcome to the depositary who shall inform all States.

3. Where an offense involves nuclear material used for peaceful purposes in domestic use, storage or transport, and both the alleged offender and the nuclear material remain in the territory of the State Party in which the offense was committed, nothing in this Convention shall be interpreted as requiring that State Party to provide information concerning criminal proceedings arising out of such an offense.

Article 15

The Annexes constitute an integral part of this Convention.

Article 16

1. A conference of States Parties shall be convened by the depositary five years after the entry into force of this Convention to review the implementation of the Convention and its adequacy as concerns the preamble, the whole of the operative part and the annexes in the light of the then prevailing situation.

2. At intervals of not less than five years thereafter, the majority of States Parties may obtain, by submitting a proposal to this effect to the depositary, the convening of further conferences with the same objective.

Article 17

1. In the event of a dispute between two or more States Parties concerning the interpretation or application of this Convention, such States Parties shall consult with a view to the settlement of the dispute by negotiation, or by any other peaceful means of settling disputes acceptable to all parties to the dispute.

2. Any dispute of this character which cannot be settled in the manner prescribed in paragraph 1 shall, at the request of any party to such dispute, be submitted to arbitration or referred to the International Court of Justice for decision. Where a dispute is submitted to arbitration, if, within six months from the date of the request, the parties to the dispute are unable to agree on the organization of the arbitration, a party may request the President of the International Court of Justice or the Secretary-General of the United Nations to appoint one or more arbitrators. In case of conflicting requests by the parties to the dispute, the request to the Secretary-General of the United Nations shall have priority.

3. Each State Party may at the time of signature, ratification, acceptance or approval of this Convention or accession thereto declare that it does not consider itself bound by either or both of the dispute settlement procedures provided for in paragraph 2. The other States Parties shall not be bound by a dispute settlement procedure provided for in paragraph 2, with respect to a State Party which has made a reservation to that procedure.

4. Any State Party which has made a reservation in accordance with paragraph 3 may at any time withdraw that reservation by notification to the depositary.

Article 18

1. This Convention shall be open for signature by all States at the Headquarters of the International Atomic Energy Agency in Vienna and at the Headquarters of the United Nations in New York from 3 March 1980 until its entry into force.

2. This Convention is subject to ratification, acceptance or approval by the signatory States.

3. After its entry into force, this Convention will be open for accession by all States.

4. (a) This Convention shall be open for signature or accession by interna-

tional organizations and regional organizations of an integration or other nature, provided that any such organization is constituted by sovereign States and has competence in respect of the negotiation, conclusion and application of international agreements in matters covered by this Convention.

(b) In matters within their competence, such organizations shall, on their own behalf, exercise the rights and fulfill the responsibilities which this Convention attributes to States Parties.

(c) When becoming party to this Convention such an organization shall communicate to the depositary a declaration indicating which States are members thereof and which articles of this Convention do not apply to it.

(d) Such an organization shall not hold any vote additional to those of its Member States.

5. Instruments of ratification, acceptance, approval or accession shall be deposited with the depositary.

Article 19

1. This Convention shall enter into force on the thirtieth day following the date of deposit of the twenty first instrument of ratification, acceptance or approval with the depositary.

2. For each State ratifying, accepting, approving or acceding to the Convention after the date of deposit of the twenty first instrument of ratification, acceptance or approval, the Convention shall enter into force on the thirtieth day after the deposit by such State of its instrument of ratification, acceptance, approval or accession.

Article 20

1. Without prejudice to article 16 a State Party may propose amendments to this Convention. The proposed amendment shall be submitted to the depositary who shall circulate it immediately to all States Parties. If a majority of States Parties request the depositary to convene a conference to consider the proposed amendments, the depositary shall invite all States Parties to attend such a conference to begin not sooner than thirty days after the invitations are issued. Any amendment adopted at the conference by a two-thirds majority of all States Parties shall be promptly circulated by the depositary to all States Parties.

2. The amendment shall enter into force for each State Party that deposits its instrument of ratification, acceptance or approval of the amendment on the thirtieth day after the date on which two thirds of the State Parties have de-

posited their instruments of ratification, acceptance or approval with the depositary. Thereafter, the amendment shall enter into force for any other State Party on the day on which that State Party deposits its instrument of ratification, acceptance or approval of the amendment.

Article 21

1. Any State Party may denounce this Convention by written notification to the depositary.

2. Denunciation shall take effect one hundred and eighty days following the date on which notification is received by the depositary.

Article 22

The depositary shall promptly notify all States of:

(a) each signature of this Convention;
(b) each deposit of an instrument of ratification, acceptance, approval or accession;
(c) any reservation or withdrawal in accordance with article 17;
(d) any communication made by an organization in accordance with paragraph 4(c) of article 18;
(e) the entry into force of this Convention;
(f) the entry into force of any amendment to this Convention; and
(g) any denunciation made under article 21.

Article 23

The original of this Convention, of which the Arabic, Chinese, English, French, Russian and Spanish texts are equally authentic, shall be deposited with the Director General of the International Atomic Energy Agency who shall send certified copies thereof to all States.

IN WITNESS WHEREOF, the undersigned, being duly authorized, have signed this Convention, opened for signature at Vienna and at New York on 3 March 1980.

Annex I

Levels of Physical Protection To Be Applied in International Transport of Nuclear Material as Categorized in Annex II

1. Levels of physical protection for nuclear material during storage incidental to international nuclear transport include:

   (a) For Category III materials, storage within an area to which access is controlled;

   (b) For Category II materials, storage within an area under constant surveillance by guards or electronic devices, surrounded by a physical barrier with a limited number of points of entry under appropriate control or any area with an equivalent level of physical protection;

   (c) For Category I material, storage within a protected area as defined for Category II above, to which, in addition, access is restricted to persons whose trustworthiness has been determined, and which is under surveillance by guards who are in close communication with appropriate response forces. Specific measures taken in this context should have as their object the detection and prevention of any assault, unauthorized access or unauthorized removal of material.

2. Levels of physical protection for nuclear material during international transport include:

   (a) For Category II and III materials, transportation shall take place under special precautions including prior arrangements among sender, receiver, and carrier, and prior agreement between natural or legal persons subject to the jurisdiction and regulation of exporting and importing States, specifying time, place and procedures for transferring transport responsibility;

   (b) For Category I materials, transportation shall take place under special precautions identified above for transportation of Category II and II materials, and in addition, under constant surveillance by escorts and under conditions which assure close communication with appropriate response forces;

   (c) For natural uranium other than in the form of ore or ore-residue, transportation protection for quantities exceeding 500 kilograms U shall include advance notification of shipment specifying mode of transport, expected time of arrival and confirmation of receipt of shipment.

Annex II

Table: Categorization of Nuclear Material

Material	Form	Category I	II	III[3]
1. Plutonium[1]	Unirradiated[2]	2 kg or more	Less than 2 kg but more than 500 g.	500 g or less but more than 15 g.
2. Uranium-235	Unirradiated[2]: —uranium enriched to 20% U^{235} or more	5 kg or more	Less than 5 kg but more than 1 kg.	1 kg or less but more than 15 g.
	—uranium enriched to 10% U^{235} but less than 20%	---------	10 kg or more	Less than 10 kg but more than 1 kg.
	—uranium enriched above natural, but less than 10% U^{235}.	----------------------	----------------------	10 kg or more.
3. Uranium-233	Unirradiated[2]	2 kg or more	Less than 2 kg but more than 500 g.	500 g or less but more than 15 g.
4. Irradiated fuel	----------------------	----------------------	Depleted or natural uranium, thorium or low-enriched fuel (less than 10% fissile content).[4,5]	

[1] All plutonium except that with isotopic concentration exceeding 80% in plutonium-238.

[2] Material not irradiated in a reactor or material irradiated in a reactor but with a radiation level equal to or less than 100 rads/hour at one metre unshielded.

[3] Quantities not falling in category III and natural uranium should be protected in accordance with prudent management practice.

[4] Although this level of protection is recommended, it would be open to States, upon evaluation of the specific circumstances, to assign a different category of physical protection.

[5] Other fuel which by virtue of its original fissile material contents is classified as Category I and II before irradiation may be reduced one category level while the radiation level from the fuel exceeds 100 rads/hour at one metre unshielded.

States that have signed or ratified the Convention on the Physical Protection of Nuclear Material as of 1 September 1985

Signatories	*Ratifications*
Australia	
Austria	
Belgium	
Brazil	
Bulgaria	x
Canada	
Czechoslovakia	x
Denmark	
Dominican Republic	
European Atomic Energy Community	
Finland	
France	
German Democratic Republic	x
Germany, Federal Republic of	
Greece	
Guatemala	x
Haiti	
Hungary	x
Ireland	
Israel	
Korea (Republic of)	x
Luxembourg	
Netherlands	
Niger	
Norway	x
Panama	
Paraguay	x
Philippines	x
Poland	x
Portugal	
Romania	
South Africa	
Sweden	x
Turkey	x
United States	x
USSR	x
United Kingdom	
Yugoslavia	
	14

Note: 21 ratifications are required for entry into force.

Appendix G: Extract from Joint Statement Issued at the Geneva Summit Meeting, November 21, 1985

Nuclear Non-Proliferation

General Secretary Gorbachev and President Reagan reaffirmed the commitment of the USSR and the U.S. to the Treaty on the Non-Proliferation of Nuclear Weapons and their interest in strengthening together with other countries the non-proliferation regime, and in further enhancing the effectiveness of the Treaty, *inter alia* by enlarging its membership.

They note with satisfaction the overall positive results of the recent Review Conference of the Treaty on the Non-Proliferation of Nuclear Weapons.

The USSR and the U.S. reaffirm their commitment, assumed by them under the Treaty on the Non-Proliferation of Nuclear Weapons, to pursue negotiations in good faith on matters of nuclear arms limitation and disarmament in accordance with Article VI of the Treaty.

The two sides plan to continue to promote the strengthening of the International Atomic Energy Agency and to support the activities of the Agency in implementing safeguards as well as in promoting the peaceful uses of nuclear energy.

They view positively the practice of regular Soviet-U.S. consultations on non-proliferation of nuclear weapons which have been businesslike and constructive and express their intent to continue this practice in the future.

Appendix H: Observations on the U.S.-China Agreement for Cooperation

As this book goes to press, the Agreement for Cooperation between the United States and the People's Republic of China on the civil uses of nuclear energy has just entered into force. The relationship of that agreement to the issues discussed in this volume is discussed below by the Rapporteur of the U.S. study.

China's non-proliferation policies and practices

In the past, the PRC has been hostile to non-proliferation efforts, made unsafeguarded nuclear exports to countries of special concern, and was emerging as a nuclear supplier that might well undermine the international non-proliferation regime. In pursuing its interest in importing foreign reactor technology, however, the Chinese entered into negotiations first with France, and then with the United States, Japan, the Federal Republic of Germany, the United Kingdom, Argentina, Brazil, and others. To varying degrees, these countries attempted in the course of their negotiations to convince the Chinese of the need to adopt more responsible nuclear export policies. In the past few years, China has joined the International Atomic Energy Agency, declared that it would not contribute to proliferation, announced that it would require IAEA safeguards on all its nuclear exports to non-nuclear weapon states, offered to discuss with the IAEA arrangements for the application of IAEA safeguards on some facilities in China, and appears to have discontinued its proliferatory activities.

Its agreements with Japan, Argentina, and Brazil provide for IAEA safeguards on all transactions thereunder, and those with the United States, the United Kingdom and the Federal Republic of Germany at least contain provisions designed to ensure that any retransfer of nuclear materials or equipment subject to the agreement by China to any non-nuclear weapon state will be subject to IAEA safeguards. None of these agreements require *full-scope* safeguards in the cooperating state (although Japan and the FRG in fact have such safeguards coverage), and the agreements with the United Kingdom, France, the United States, and the Federal Republic of Germany make no provision for IAEA safeguards in China.

Congressional consideration of the U.S. agreement was long deferred pending clarification of a number of issues that had arisen over Chinese nuclear exports and assistance to states of special proliferation concern, and this was one of the principal issues during the Congressional review process. Both the administration and a majority of the Congress appeared satisfied that China has terminated its most egregious activities of this kind and pointed to the fact that under the Nuclear Non-Proliferation Act of 1978 any resumption of such proliferatory activities by China would preclude further cooperation under the agreement. The administration stated that the Chinese were fully aware of this fact, and the joint resolution of approval of the agreement calls for a Presidential certification, before actual exports take place under the agreement, that no intervening activities by the Chinese have taken place that would activate that provision. The administration also argued that the agreement will give us a continuing opportunity to influence Chinese behavior in this field and give the Chinese a greater stake in conforming with international norms.

Criticisms of the agreement

The principal criticisms of the agreement itself were (a) that it did not provide for IAEA safeguards or their equivalent on U.S. exports under the agreement; (b) that the language relied upon as satisfying the statutory requirement for a U.S. right of prior consent over reprocessing was defective and ambiguous; and (c) that one clause in the agreement raised questions as to whether future changes in U.S. laws and regulations would be applied to this agreement. There was concern not only over the impact of these provisions on our cooperation with China, but also over the risk that they might be used as a precedent for further agreements (and there was evidence suggesting that the latter concern was not groundless). Concern was also expressed that they could lead to future disputes with the Chinese.

The administration pointed out that neither the NPT nor the U.S. legislation requires IAEA safeguards on transfers to nuclear weapon states; that the agreement does contemplate the negotiation of arrangements to help verify compliance with the basic Chinese guarantees under the agreement; and that the results of these negotiations can be judged at the export licensing stage. They also referred to the Chinese voluntary offer, announced in September 1985, to negotiate an agreement for the application of safeguards to some facilities in China, and at least one witness urged that a major effort be made by the United States to persuade the Chinese to include under the coverage of that agreement materials and equipment acquired pursuant to the U.S. agreement for cooperation. (Such an arrangement has been made by the United States, under its voluntary safeguards agreement, for imports from Canada and Australia.) This would help meet objections that the special treatment of China would make it more difficult to bring about full-scope safeguards coverage in non-nuclear weapon states. (India has been particularly critical of the double standard evidenced by this agreement.)

On the consent right over reprocessing (which included a clause saying that future Chinese requests for reprocessing consent were to be "favorably" considered), while the administration insisted that it met the statutory requirement, there was a concern that it could lead to future disagreements with the Chinese and consensus that it would not be acceptable in future agreements. The joint resolution addressed the first of these concerns by making clear the U.S. understanding that "the obligation to consider favorably a request to carry out activities described in Article 5 (2) of the Agreement shall not prejudice the decision of the United States to approve or disapprove such a request."

Several witnesses noted that the Chinese would not be in a position to reprocess any spent fuel derived from cooperation under this agreement until approximately the year 2000, and one witness noted that the Chinese had ample other sources of weapons-usable material, which was not the pacing item in the Chinese military program, and that if the U.S. Agreement were not permitted to go into effect, the Chinese could procure such material and equipment from other suppliers who did not insist on any such consent rights.

To protect against the use of this (and other criticized provisions of the agreement) as a precedent, a joint resolution expressing approval of the agreement stated that such approval was "notwithstanding section 123 of the Atomic Energy Act"—indicating that its sponsors did not agree with the administration's position that the provisions of the agreement fully satisfied the criteria in that section for new agreements for cooperation—and explicitly provided that "Nothing in the Agreement or this resolution may be construed as providing a precedent or other basis for the negotiation or renegotiation of any other agreement for cooperation."

With respect to the third of the criticized provisions, the administration provided assurances that it would comply with future legislation even if this created questions of its compliance with its obligations under this agreement, and the joint resolution provides that "Each proposed export pursuant to this agreement will be subject to the United States laws and regulations in effect at the time of each such export."

Net assessment

While the text of the agreement includes some undesirable deviations from other recent nuclear cooperation agreements, and future Chinese behavior in this field cannot be predicted with assurance, the agreement is basically a framework for cooperation and contains no actual obligations to make exports to China. Such actual exports will be subject to the licensing process, at which time assessments can be made both of the verification arrangements worked out under the agreement and the degree to which the favorable changes in Chinese policies towards non-proliferation are still being followed. The agreement also gives the United States opportunities to influence Chinese policy on this subject that we would not have in the absence of the agreement.

Appendix I: Proceedings of the two panels and acknowledgments

The provenance of the U.S. report included a series of panel discussions held between November 1982 and November 1985, stimulated by case studies and other background papers prepared by staff and (in some cases) presentations by guest speakers; a meeting with representatives of the Japan Institute of Foreign Affairs (Ambassador Kinya Niiseki, Chairman, and Mr. Kumao Kaneko, Director of Research Coordination); and a two-and-a-half day joint meeting of the U.S. and West European groups held in Washington, D.C., in December 1984. Seven members of the U.S. panel, under the leadership of Warren Christopher, also held two days of consultations in Moscow in November 1984 with a group assembled by the Soviet Academy of Sciences, under the chairmanship of its Vice President Velikhov, and met with U.S. Ambassador to the USSR Arthur Hartman. Several panel members obtained further insights from private discussions with individuals from the countries studied.

The work of the European panel included a series of discussions by its Steering Committee in 1983–85 and a briefing by Nelson Sievering, Deputy Director General of the International Atomic Energy Agency; the in-depth case studies and regional workshops referred to in the Introduction to its report; and the joint meeting with the U.S. panel in December, 1984, in which many of the following authors of commissioned papers, as well as members of the Steering Committee, participated:

Dieter Braun, Stiftung Wissenschaft und Politik, Ebenhausen, FRG
Maurizio Cremasco, Istituto Affari Internazionali, Rome
Akbar Etemad, Energium, Paris
Julien Goens, Centre d'Études d'Essais Nucléaires, Brussels
Wolf Grabendorff, Institute for European-Latin American Relations, Madrid
David Hart, University of East Anglia, United Kingdom
Cesare Merlini, Istituto Affari Internazionali, Rome
Antonio Sanchez-Gijon, Instituto de Cuestiónes Internacionales, Madrid
Ben Soetendorp, Rijksuniversiteit te Leiden, The Netherlands
Marian van Leeuwen, Nederlands Instituut voor Internationale Betrekkingen, The Hague

The summary report of the European group was first published in Europe by the Centre for European Policy Studies, with whose permission it is reprinted herein. Selected working papers of both panels are being published separately.

This project was made possible by generous grants to the U.S. panel by the McKnight Foundation and an individual donor, and to both panels by the

Ford Foundation and the Rockefeller Brothers Fund, to all of whom we are grateful not only for such funding but also for the keen interest they have shown in the substance of the project. The participants are also grateful to the Council on Foreign Relations and the Centre for European Policy Studies, which were the institutional bases for this project, and to the supremely competent and helpful staffs of both organizations.

The U.S. panel also wishes to acknowledge the valuable contributions of the following persons, without any implication that they necessarily share the views expressed in its Summary Report: former panel members John Culver and Arnold Kramish and the following guest speakers and discussants: Senator Charles McC. Mathias, Jr.; Ambassador-at-Large Richard T. Kennedy; Ambassadors William Edmondson and Lewis Dunn; Hans Heymann; Philip Stoddard; Myron Kratzer; Joseph Yager, Sidney Sober, Rodney Jones, Jeremy Stone, Dimitri Simes, Kim Elliott, and William C. Potter.

Appendix J: Members of the two panels

Members of U.S. Panel

Gerard C. Smith (Chairman) is President of The Consultants International Group, Inc., and Chairman of the Board of Directors of The Arms Control Association; formerly he served as Director, U.S. Arms Control and Disarmament Agency, and chief of the U.S. Delegation to the Strategic Arms Limitation Talks (SALT I); the President's Special Representative for Non-Proliferation Matters and U.S. Representative to the International Atomic Energy Agency; Assistant Secretary of State and Director of the Policy Planning Staff, U.S. Department of State.

Robert A. Charpie (Vice Chairman) is President of Cabot Corporation and formerly served as Director, Reactor Division, Oak Ridge National Laboratories; Director of Technology and President of the Electronics Division of Union Carbide; President of Bell & Howell; a member of the General Advisory Committee, U.S. Atomic Energy Commission; and a member of the National Science Board.

Alton Frye (Co-Director) is Washington Director of the Council on Foreign Relations, and formerly served as Legislative and Administrative Assistant to Senator Brooke.

J. Robert Schaetzel (Co-Director) is a consultant who formerly served as U.S. Representative to the European Communities.

L. Dean Brown is President of the Middle East Institute and formerly served as U.S. Ambassador to Jordan, Senegal, and Gambia.

Albert Carnesale is Professor of Public Policy at Harvard University's John F. Kennedy School of Government and a consultant to several agencies of the U.S. government. A nuclear engineer by training, he served on the U.S. delegation to the Strategic Arms Limitation Talks (SALT I) and the International Nuclear Fuel Cycle Evaluation.

Warren Christopher is Chairman, O'Melveny and Myers, and formerly served as Deputy Secretary of State and Deputy Attorney General of the United States.

John Hugh Crimmins is a consultant who formerly served as U.S. Ambassador to Brazil and the Dominican Republic.

Warren Donnelly is a Senior Specialist, Congressional Research Service, Library of Congress, who participated in the panel as an ex-officio observer.

Philip J. Farley has been involved in non-proliferation efforts since the 1950s, when as a State Department official he had an active role in implementing the U.S. "Atoms for Peace" program, in organizing the International Atomic Energy Agency, and in the management of the initial nuclear test ban negotiations. He served as Deputy Director of the U.S. Arms Control and Disarmament Agency and Alternate Chairman of the U.S. delegation to SALT I negotiations, and as Deputy U.S. Special Representative for Non-Proliferation Matters.

Ellen Frost is Director of Japan Relations for Westinghouse Electric Corporation and formerly served as Deputy Assistant Secretary of Defense for International Affairs.

Mark Garrison is Director, Center for Foreign Policy Development, Brown University, and formerly served as Minister-Counselor, U.S. Embassy, Moscow.

William Gleysteen is a former Foreign Service Officer who served as U.S. Ambassador to the Republic of Korea.

Robert Goheen is President Emeritus of Princeton University and a Senior Fellow, Woodrow Wilson School of Public and International Affairs, and formerly served as U.S. Ambassador to India.

Benjamin Huberman is Vice President, The Consultants International Group, Inc., and formerly served as Deputy Director, White House Office of Science and Technology Policy, senior staff member of the National Security Council, and Director, Office of Policy Evaluation, Nuclear Regulatory Commission.

Spurgeon M. Keeny, Jr. is President and Executive Director of The Arms Control Association, and formerly served as Deputy Director, U.S. Arms Control and Disarmament Agency; senior staff member, National Security Council; Chairman, Nuclear Energy Policy Study, Ford Foundation; and Scholar in Residence, National Academy of Sciences.

Andrew Pierre is a Senior Fellow and Director, Project on European-American Relations, at the Council on Foreign Relations, and a former Foreign Service Officer. Formerly on the staff of the Brookings Institution and the Hudson Institute, he has also taught at Columbia University.

Robert V. Roosa is a partner in Brown Brothers, Harriman & Co., and formerly served as Under Secretary for Monetary Affairs, U.S. Treasury.

James R. Schlesinger is Counselor, The Georgetown Center for Strategic and International Studies, and formerly served as Secretary of Defense, Secretary of Energy, Director of Central Intelligence, and Chairman of the U.S. Atomic Energy Commission.

Lt. Gen. Brent Scowcroft is a consultant, who formerly served as Assistant to the President for National Security Affairs.

Marshall Shulman is Director of the W. Averell Harriman Institute for the Advanced Study of the Soviet Union, Columbia University.

Samuel F. Wells, Jr., is Associate Director of the Woodrow Wilson International Center for Scholars, and directs its European Institute.

Charles N. Van Doren (Executive Director and Rapporteur), formerly served as Assistant Director for Non-Proliferation, U.S. Arms Control and Disarmament Agency.

Note: The views in the Summary Report reflect solely those of the panel and not necessarily those of the organizations with which its members are shown above to be affiliated.

Members of the European (NANPEA) Steering Committee

Johan Jørgen Holst, the chairman of the NANPEA Steering Committee, is director of the Norwegian Institute of International Affairs, and a member of the Council of the Centre for European Policy Studies, the Executive Committee and Council of the International Institute for Strategic Studies, the Board of Directors of the Institute for East-West Security Studies, and the Trilateral Commission. He is also scientific consultant to the Independent Commission on Disarmament and Security Issues, special advisor to the Chairman of the World Commission on Environment and Development, a member of the steering group of the European Security Study (ESECS), and a consultant to the Ford Foundation. Before taking the post of Director of the NIIA, Mr. Holst served as Minister of State in the Norwegian Ministries of Foreign Affairs and Defence. His numerous publications include books on foreign policy, East-West relations, strategic issues, arms control, Nordic security, and regional cooperation.

Sergio Finzi is Director of Nuclear Research and Development (DG XII) at the Commission of the European Communities. His previous positions included Director of the Programmes Management, Engineering, and Applied Science and Technology Departments at the Joint Research Centre's establishment of ISPRA. Prior to that he was Scientific Officer to Euratom's Directorate-General for Research and Development and head of Euratom's Technology Division. Mr. Finzi is the author of many publications in the fields of safety of thermal and fast reactors, storage of radioactive waste, safeguards of fissile materials, etc.

David Fischer joined the International Atomic Energy Agency in the late 1950s and was Assistant Director-General upon his retirement in 1982. Prior to joining the IAEA he was in the South African Diplomatic Service. Mr. Fischer has participated in several international research projects on non-proliferation. He is the author of a recent book on safeguards and of many articles on the non-proliferation regime and the IAEA.

Bertrand Goldschmidt, currently advisor to the OECD's Nuclear Energy Agency, was French Governor on the Board of the IAEA and its Chairman in 1980. One of the founders of the French Atomic Energy Commission, Mr. Goldschmidt was in charge of its International Relations Division and its Chemistry Division. During World War II he was a member of the British team participating in the atomic projects in North America. Mr. Goldschmidt has written several books and many essays on the history of nuclear energy and non-proliferation.

Simone Herpels, who has been awarded the "Officer of the Order of Leopold", is Head of the Scientific Service in the Belgian Ministry of Foreign Affairs. She began her career there and has held a number of posts, including working for the Commissioner of the Atomic Energy Department and the Secretary of the Belgian Delegation to the UN General Assembly. Miss Herpels has participated in numerous conferences and meetings of the IAEA, Euratom, the London Suppliers Group, and the Zangger Committee on nuclear problems, the development of peaceful uses for nuclear energy, etc.

Guenter Hildenbrand is a Senior Vice President and Group Executive of Kraftwerk Union AG, the leading supplier of nuclear facilities and equipment in the Federal Republic of Germany. Having trained as a physicist, he is responsible for KWU's activities in the nuclear fuel cycle in both the national and international context. Mr. Hildenbrand has participated in a number of international conferences, workshops, and project groups dealing with nuclear energy and non-proliferation issues.

Giorgio La Malfa is Chairman of the Foreign Affairs Committee of the Italian Chamber of Deputies and Deputy Secretary of the Republican Party. From 1980 to 1982 he served as Minister of the Budget and Economic Planning. Mr. La Malfa is also a Professor of Economic Policy, Chairman of CEEP, an institute for research on economic policy, and co-editor of *Energia e Materie Prime,* a bimonthly journal on energy and raw materials.

Peter Ludlow is Director of the Centre for European Policy Studies. Formerly Professor of History at the European University Institute, Florence, he is the author of numerous books and articles on international history and politics in the 20th century, including *The Wartime Alliance and Development of European Integration and Cooperation.*

Sir Ronald Mason is the UK member of the UN Secretary-General's Commission on Disarmament, an international lecturer on western defence policies, a consultant on strategic issues, and a professor of chemical physics. A Knight Commander of Bath and a Fellow of the Royal Society, in 1983 he was awarded the US Department of Energy Distinguished Associate Award. Sir Ronald has held numerous public appointments, including Chief Scientific Advisor to the UK Ministry of Defence and Chairman of the Science Board of the UK Science Research Council.

Harald Müller is a CEPS Research Fellow and Executive Director of the CEPS project "New Approaches to Non-Proliferation: A European Approach" (NANPEA). He is also a research fellow and a member of the Foundation Council of the Peace Research Institute Frankfurt and a visiting professor at the Johns Hopkins University Center for International Relations in Bologna. Mr. Müller has written several books and articles on nuclear proliferation, arms control, and energy and security.

Angel Viñas is Professor of Economics at the University of Madrid and Professor of International Economic Relations at the Spanish Diplomatic School. A member of the Spanish Socialist Party (PSOE), he serves as an advisor to the Minister of Foreign Affairs. Mr. Viñas is the author of many books and articles on Spanish foreign policy, international economic policy, and security issues.

Unless otherwise indicated, the views expressed in this report are attributable only to authors in a personal capacity and not to any institution.

Council on Foreign Relations

Founded in 1921, the Council on Foreign Relations is an educational institution, a research institution, and a unique forum bringing together leaders from the academic, public, and private worlds. The Council's basic constituency is its members, but it also reaches out to the broader public so as to contribute to the national dialogue on foreign policy. The Council is private and nonpartisan and takes no positions as an organization.

The Council conducts meetings that give its members an opportunity to talk with invited guests from the United States and abroad who have special experience and expertise in international affairs. Its study program explores foreign policy questions through research by the Council's professional staff, visiting Fellows, and others, and through study groups and conferences. The Council also publishes the journal, *Foreign Affairs,* in addition to books and monographs. It is affiliated with thirty-eight Committees on Foreign Relations located around the country and maintains a Corporation Service Program that provides meetings and other services for its approximately 200 corporate subscribers.

Centre for European Policy Studies (CEPS)

The Centre for European Policy Studies (CEPS) is a non-profit, nonpartisan, and independent research institute that focuses on the major medium- and long-term issues facing the European Communities and Western Europe, both internally and internationally. Through the Centre's Advanced Policy Forum, representatives of government, industry, the trade unions, academia, and other fields affecting and affected by public policy join together for the study, discussion, and proposal of policy alternatives.

The core of the Centre's research work is constituted by a series of programmes covering economic and social affairs, foreign policy and security questions, and political and institutional problems. CEPS publications stem from this work, but remain the responsibility of the authors concerned. Information about membership in the Centre and subscriptions to its wide range of publications may be obtained from the Membership and Publications Secretaries at the Centre for European Policy Studies, rue Ducale 33, B–1000 Brussels, or from CEPS-US, 200 East 33rd Street, Suite 26G, New York, N.Y. 10016.